PRAISE FOR *EMOTIONS!*

Dr. Mary Lamia has written an exceptional book about emotions. Written in lucid prose, readers will feel as if they are engaged in a conversation with Dr. Lamia. The reader can follow the thread of a personal emotion by naming it and then reading the informative chapter on it. Themes that have been distressing can be seen in a new light and this will lead to making better choices about relationships with others. Readers of this book will learn to use their own emotions wisely. I highly recommend *Emotions! Making Sense of Your Feelings.*

—Mardi Horowitz, MD
Distinguished Professor of Psychiatry,
University of California San Francisco

A veteran and highly respected psychologist, Dr. Mary Lamia provides her readers with an important and illuminating understanding not only of their own emotions but those of others with whom they interact. A practical, lucid book, *Emotions! Making Sense of Your Feelings* helps to unlock many of the mysteries and vexing challenges of emotions and their effect on us and, perhaps most important of all, the wisdom of how best to deal with them.

—Michael Krasny
Host of *Forum* on KQED-FM, San Francisco;
Professor at San Francisco State University

Mary Lamia, in her book *Emotions!* guides her readers through a sea of emotions, explaining them in great detail while using real life experiences in every chapter. As a teenager in high school, I am exposed to a full range of emotions at any given time, and Dr. Lamia's book helps me make sense of those feelings and understand them from a different perspective through examples that relate to my life. The book highlights our everyday feelings and illustrates the effects they have on our lives and behavior, and gives the reader practical tools to deal with them effectively in a more positive and constructive way. You can pick up *Emotions!* and read any chapter on its own and find it really beneficial. I recommend this book to teens and adults who encounter any source of stress or frustration in their lives. It is equally helpful for those individuals who are curious about learning more about emotions and how to deal with them more effectively.

—Alex Jutrzonka
High school student, happiness blogger,
and aspiring psychologist

Emotions! Making Sense of Your Feelings explains the inner workings of the array of emotions teens experience. Understandable, concise, and informative, this book is a great reference for teens to fully understand any and all emotions they might be feeling. It provides an anatomical overview of how emotions affect teens physiologically, and delves into social situations that are prevalent in teen life. The book is an excellent guide for teenagers who seek to understand what they're feeling, why they're feeling it, and how to cope.

—Lena Felton
High school student

Emotions! Making Sense of Your Feelings is an extensively researched book chock full of interesting facts and studies. From the beginning, it is very clear and it lucidly defines the plethora of terms surrounding this complex topic. Dr. Mary Lamia does a great job of distinguishing the reality about emotions from the way that they are culturally perceived. This book also answers the question of *why* we experience these emotions from an evolutionary perspective. It was informative and gave me tools to think about these issues in my daily life.

—Henry Kinder
High school student

EMOTIONS!

MAKING SENSE
OF YOUR FEELINGS

by Mary Lamia, PhD

Magination Press • Washington, DC
American Psychological Association

Published by
MAGINATION PRESS
An Educational Publishing Foundation Book
American Psychological Association
750 First Street, NE
Washington, DC 20002

For more information about our books, including a complete catalog, please write to us, call 1-800-374-2721, or visit our website at www.apa.org/pubs/magination.

Cover design by Oliver Munday
Typeset by Circle Graphics, Columbia, MD
Printed by United Book Press, Inc., Baltimore, MD

Library of Congress Cataloging-in-Publication Data
Lamia, Mary C.
  Emotions! : making sense of your feelings / by Mary Lamia.
     p. cm.
  Includes bibliographical references and index.
  ISBN 978-1-4338-1193-7 (pbk. : alk. paper) 1. Emotions—Juvenile literature. I. Title.
  BF561.L355 2012
  152.4—dc23
                          2012016190

Manufactured in the United States of America

First printing — June 2012

10 9 8 7 6 5 4 3 2 1

CONTENTS

Contents

INTRODUCTION

When I began writing this book about emotions I discovered just how much there is to know about the subject. Understanding your emotions is essential, considering how significantly emotions inform you, affect the decisions you make, determine the ways in which you might respond to situations, and how they can motivate you to reach your goals. Knowing how to interpret and respond to your emotions will give you an advantage socially, academically, and personally. Emotions contribute significantly to your intelligence and your ability to navigate through your life. Simply based on some of the research studies summarized in the various chapters of this book, you will learn that:

- Focusing on feelings instead of details may lead to better quality decision making for certain complex decisions.
- Anxiety can improve creativity, productivity, and the quality of your work.
- In competitive situations, fear can interfere with success if it causes you to change your strategy.
- Your friend's embarrassing behavior won't reflect on you.

- People who bully do not have low self-esteem; however, they are very shame-prone.
- Guilt helps you to maintain your relationships.
- Showing the pride you have in achievements can help you socially.
- Lonely people look for sources of acceptance in facial expressions.
- Hope can affect expectation and how you feel.
- Many people cry at a happy ending after holding back their expression of sadness.
- Venting anger doesn't help you.
- Spiders may be more disgusting than frightening.
- Envy leads people to focus on the details of those they envy.
- When focusing on reading material for a test, pay attention to unappealing sentences.
- Overvaluing happiness can possibly lead you to be less happy, even when happiness is within your reach.

You don't necessarily have to read this book cover to cover. Depending on what you're experiencing, you can choose a chapter that resonates with you. If you are anxious you might want to read Chapter 2, "Anxiety Is Your Friend," which will help you gain some perspective on what you're feeling. If envy is consuming you at the moment, you may benefit from reading about it in Chapter 13, "The Secret Life of Envy." Maybe you're dealing with an embarrassment or shame. You might want to read Chapter 4, "Embarrassment: Being Noticed With Regret" as well as Chapter 5, "Hiding From Shame." Perhaps an important relationship is over and you're experiencing sadness. In that case, Chapter 10, "Sadness and Sad Love," may resonate with you.

Likely you'll want to know how a particular emotion applies to your life and perhaps what you can do to recover when an emotion is intensely experienced. To help you with this, each of the chapters on specific emotions will include a section titled "What's It to You?" In addition, each chapter will provide an example of the emotion in a particular context and will include research studies about the specific emotion covered that may be relevant to your everyday life.

Imagine having a tool that can improve your motivation, self-awareness, social relationships, decision-making skills, self-control, and your ability to achieve goals. Understanding your emotions can do all of that for you. So let's begin.

CHAPTER 1

EMOTIONS: THE BASICS ARE ALL IN YOUR HEAD

Emotions are a particular information system—a summary of information about the environment and an aggregate of a huge amount of data about a situation. They are indicators to interpret and use rather than annoyances to try to ignore or control. You may think that the best course of action is to suppress or ignore an intense emotion rather than figure it out. But why ignore an emotion that has evolved over thousands of years to help you?

Although emotions are felt in your body, they originate in your brain. Your brain has the ability to size up circumstances in the environment and automatically and unconsciously create an emotional response. There's a lot of stimulation in your life to reflect upon and so you are constantly faced with an abundance of information that you must process. You don't have time to consider all of that information and process it in a reflective fashion, but your brain processes it for you passively and unconsciously—without your awareness. If your brain comes across something it evaluates as needing your attention, an emotion will be triggered and you'll be sent a general but vague signal in the form of the feelings and thoughts that are created by the emotion. Beyond alerting you to pay attention, physiological changes associated with your emotions motivate and prepare you to take action. So emotions are immediate and reflexive based on your brain's evaluation of a specific situation, event, thought, or stimulus. They serve a purpose, informing you, the operator of your body, what to do. In this way, your emotions serve as a cueing system—an attention-directing system associated with physiological changes that can motivate and prepare you to take action.

Granted, the system can have false alarms, such as when an emotion that was triggered in a similar circumstance in your past becomes activated in a current situation. Even so, your brain is doing an amazing job of integrating memories of past emotional experiences in order to evaluate subsequent situations and decide upon the emotion that should be activated. And impressively, it all happens instantaneously and without your conscious knowledge. For example, if you dated a person with green eyes who ended up betraying you in some way, your emotional system may unnecessarily warn you by making you anxious if you become infatuated with another person who has green eyes. Thus you need to consciously evaluate your emotional responses to determine if they are appropriate or an emotional misfire.

FEELING AND THINKING YOUR EMOTIONS

An emotional response is experienced physiologically as a feeling in your body. Feelings are created by signals sent from your brain that activate your *autonomic* and *central nervous systems*. These systems are responsible for affecting your muscles and organs. Your *autonomic sympathetic nervous system,* for example, knows how to boost your heart rate, cause your hands to sweat, and make your mouth dry, which you've likely felt when you're anxious. When you experience fear, your sympathetic nervous system creates what's considered to be "fight or flight" responses. In contrast, your *autonomic parasympathetic nervous system* can lower your heart rate and help you rest, as it does when you experience emotions such as sadness, disgust, or interest.

Emotions not only create sensations in your body, they also lead you to form *cognitions*—thoughts that give your emotions a context. As a result, anger makes you feel hot, tense, and irritable, and causes you to think negatively. Disgust can make you feel sick to your stomach and can lead you to think something is dirty or contaminated. Sadness creates a heavy feeling in your chest and leads you to think unhappy thoughts. Thoughts are produced initially by an emotional response, and further *affects*—the experiences of emotion or feeling—can then be produced by the thoughts themselves (Lerner & Keltner, 2000). Put another way, your emotions can lead to cognitions, and your cognitions can create emotions (Lazarus, 1984; M. Lewis, 2008; Zajonc, 1984). So what do you think the impact would be of thinking negatively or ruminating about something that made you angry, worried, or sad?

APPRAISING EXPERIENCES

Without any conscious or deliberate effort on your part, your brain evaluates every situation you encounter and decides if an emotion should be activated to help you. The ability of your brain to evaluate situations, events, or stimuli is referred to as an *appraisal* or an *appraisal tendency*. A situation may have a particular meaning for you, and therefore your brain appraises the situation in terms of what emotion it will create. Such appraisals happen automatically, without your conscious control, and trigger a reflexive response (Winkielman, Zajonc, & Schwartz, 1997; Zajonc, 1980). The part of the human brain responsible for appraisals is the *amygdala,* which is an almond-shaped region in the mid-brain (LeDoux, 1996). Your appraisal system takes into account your well-being, plans, and goals when it processes events or situations and provides them with meaning (Levenson, 1994).

How such appraisals develop is somewhat controversial. Are we hard-wired to experience certain emotions as a result of specific circumstances, or do our early experiences with emotions and the memories they formed lead us to evaluate future situations in particular ways? Since emotions serve to protect humans by helping them to respond to situations, then perhaps appraisals that activate emotions can result both from our innate ability to size up situations as well as what we've learned from past experiences. As you will read in a later chapter, the emotion of disgust appears to involve both possibilities; for example, the smell of spoiled milk can make you disgusted, but your disgust might also be triggered by seeing that the expiration date on the milk was two weeks ago and recalling how you felt when you drank spoiled milk in the past.

Researchers who theorize that memory is what contributes most to our emotional responses to situations assume that we appraise events—both consciously and unconsciously—based on how closely the circumstance resembles past situations (Clore & Ortony, 2008; LeDoux, 1996). As a result, certain situations are consistently sources of emotions that you have connected with them in the past, and these are considered to be *appraisal tendencies*—the characteristic way in which your brain has learned to evaluate specific situations.

TAKING ACTION

Once your brain has instantaneously processed an event or a situation and provided it with meaning, it activates an emotion that will prepare you to take action. The result of your brain's appraisal of a situation is designated as an *action tendency,* which consists of reflexive urges and behavioral responses to a particular emotion (Clore & Ortony, 2008; Fredrickson & Cohn, 2008; Lazarus, 1994; LeDoux, 1996). In action tendencies, the amygdala is involved in triggering the release of hormones related to high stress, such as epinephrine (adrenaline) and gluco-corticoids from the adrenal gland, which can lead to either an enhancement of memory or an impairment of memory for an event (LeDoux & Phelps, 2008). Thus, if your brain appraises a situation as dangerous—for example, you're walking on a narrow trail and see a coiled up poisonous snake ahead of you—it will activate fear that is accompanied by the urge to respond with a particular action, such as escape or avoidance. However, once you experience the particular urge to respond, you also have the ability to cognitively consider this action tendency. In the case of seeing the snake, instead of running you may decide to back away slowly in order to avoid the danger you perceive. Since you experienced fear, your emotional memory of the event may cause you to become more vigilant as you continue walking.

Appraisals that trigger emotions, the resulting action tendencies, and the thoughts you might have in response are important to consider when it comes to dealing with emotions. Although you may have an inclination to take action by responding impulsively, you also have the ability to inhibit or alter a response. Since you can quickly consider the consequences of your actions, the best approach to dealing with an intense emotion is to involve some quick cognitive assessment of what would be your best approach, such as backing away instead of running in the example above. Taking into consideration the emotion that is triggered and thinking about your response to a situation before you act is what's often referred to as regulating or managing your emotions.

MAKING DECISIONS

Your emotional system can give you an advantage in your decision making if you make proper use of it. A great number of your decisions are influenced by your emotional responses because emotions are designed to evaluate and summarize experiences and inform your actions. Thus, emotions provide information about your circumstances in a simple, quick way that does not involve a lot of cognition (thinking about it). They attempt to tell you if a situation is optimal or not aligned with your goal, and how you might approach it.

So, should you trust your feelings when making a decision or not? Assuming you are fortunate enough to have choices, such as which class to take, whom to date, or whether or not to buy a particular cell phone, what approach do you use to make such decisions? At times you may focus on your feelings regarding your options and make the decision based on what feels best to you; that is, you would use your intuition. But at other times your decision making is more cognitive as you deliberate over—consciously reflect upon—various factors that are held in your memory in order to make the best choice. Another model, which is called a *dual process theory,* indicates that there are multiple sources of information to consider in decision making that may be either deliberative or affective (Epstein, 1994; Osman, 2004).

Researchers compared these decision strategies and found that focusing on feelings instead of details led to better decision quality for certain complex decisions (Mikels, Maglio, Reed, & Kaplowitz, 2011). In addition, the researchers found that deliberative processes could sometimes interfere with using emotion for decision making if over-thinking the decision occurred. The basic conclusion of the research was that when the going gets tough, use your gut feelings and don't over-think your decision.

ARE THERE BASIC EMOTIONS?

At present there is not an agreed upon classification of emotions. A comprehensive study by psychologist Paul Ekman was based upon cross-cultural consensus regarding the corresponding facial expressions of emotions. Facial expressions are emotional signals to others that reveal information about what a person is feeling, thereby providing another purpose of emotions. Ekman (1992) obtained evidence for the basic emotions of happiness, surprise, fear, sadness, anger, disgust, and contempt. Shame and interest were also studied and accepted by some researchers as having a universal facial expression (Tomkins & McCarter, 1964). Later, Ekman (1999) added to the list of basic emotions, some of which do not have universal signals, and he included shame, guilt, pride in achievement, embarrassment, excitement, contentment, sensory pleasure, satisfaction, relief, and amusement.

EMOTION STATES AND TRAITS

An emotion can last for a few seconds or a few hours (Ekman, 1994; Izard, 1993). Some authors make a distinction between an *emotion state* in which an emotion is momentary and specific to a situation, and an *emotion trait*, which has to do with the tendency of a person to exhibit a particular emotion. In other words, emotion traits are enduring tendencies you might have to experience particular emotions (Cattell & Scheier, 1961; Izard, 1991; Lerner & Keltner, 2001). An example of an emotion state might be a situation where a friend does something that makes you angry. However, if you are always prone to become angry, then anger may be an emotion trait of yours and you may be more likely to appraise a situation in a way that triggers anger because of this basic disposition that developed as a result of past experiences. Thus, you may experience certain emotional states more often, and with more intensity, due to having that same emotion trait.

A WORD ABOUT POSITIVE AND NEGATIVE EMOTIONS

Emotions are often described as positive—such as joy or excitement—or negative—such as anger or fear—based on how they make you feel. However, technically speaking, such descriptions of emotions do not necessarily apply. Consider that the point of an emotion is to provide you with information, and thus an emotion you might regard as negative would be deemed positive if it enabled you to protect yourself in a given situation. Conversely, a positive emotion such as excitement might be regarded as negative if it led you to engage in risky behavior or if it was not interpreted or managed properly.

Emotions that elevate your mood, such as pride, hope, happiness, or interest, are considered to be positive because they lift your spirits and may motivate you to pursue your goals. Certain characteristics are related to positive affect including confidence, likability, sociability, flexibility, energy, pro-social behavior, effective coping with challenge and stress, and physical well-being (Lyubomirsky, King, & Diener, 2005). Studies of resilience have found that people use positive emotions to help them recover from stressful experiences, and that positive emotions contribute to efficient emotion regulation by finding positive meaning in negative circumstances (Tugade & Fredrickson, 2004).

Positive emotions are often experienced in circumstances where things are going well. Their immediate effects broaden the range of your attention, cognition, and behaviors, while long-term effects serve to build resources that contribute to health, happiness, and survival (Fredrickson & Cohn, 2008). Positive moods have been shown to motivate people to continue pursuit of a certain action or line of thinking that they have initiated (Clore, 1994).

Can positive emotions keep you healthy? Negative emotions such as anger, anxiety, and depression are associated with behaviors that are harmful to your health, such as excessive smoking or alcohol consumption and greater body mass, and positive emotions have been found to be associated with decreased likelihood of diseases such as hypertension and diabetes mellitus (Richman, Kubzansky, Maselko, Kawachi, Choo, & Bauer, 2005). However, even though positive emotions may be protective, their association with greater health does not imply that they cause you to be healthier. Such associations may indicate instead, for example, that people who take care of themselves feel more positive in their emotional life (Richman et al., 2005). But whatever might be the case, a healthy lifestyle may involve taking good care of yourself as well as thinking positively.

SUMMARY AND CONCLUSION

Emotions instantly evaluate your experiences and inform your actions by creating physiological arousal that motivates you to take action. Although an emotion, once activated, can lead you to have certain thoughts, your cognitions can also trigger an emotional response. The feelings involved in emotional expressions motivate you to pursue a specific goal or direction, and they also send a signal to others. Although technically emotions are not positive or negative, since all emotions serve a purpose to provide information and inform your actions, emotions that enhance positive feelings about yourself have been shown to also have a positive effect on people's lives.

The following chapters will cover some specific emotions. They will be discussed in the various contexts in which you might experience them. First, we'll take a look at anxiety. And although you may want to avoid experiencing it, I hope you'll discover that anxiety is your friend.

CHAPTER **2**

ANXIETY IS YOUR FRIEND

You are leaving the house, hoping you'll run into the person with whom you are totally infatuated. You head down the street and suddenly wonder if you locked the front door. Since no one else was at home when you left, you begin to worry about locking it. If you think about why your anxiety was triggered, it may be that your brain is alerting you to the fact that you usually lock the door and this time you didn't. On the other hand, as you walked down the street you had started thinking about seeing the person you really like. Anxiety was triggered in your brain and you could be attributing that anxiety to the door being left unlocked rather than to seeing that person. You go back to check the door, find it locked, and then wonder if you are obsessive compulsive. But you aren't, since such responses to anxiety are normal. However, at the extreme, certain responses to anxiety—such as going back six times to see if the door is locked—can be a symptom of an emotion that is disordered. Eventually you realize that you are just anxiously anticipating seeing the person you like so much, and calm yourself down with the thought that you feel pretty good about yourself this morning and wouldn't mind running into anyone.

Anxiety is a vague warning sign that makes you think and feel as though something is about to happen for which you must

take action. This emotion creates arousal that you might experience in the form of nervous tension, excitement, or difficulty
with resting or sleeping. Anxiety can also lead you to be *hyper-
vigilant*—very watchful, alert, careful, or cautious. Since anxiety is triggered when your brain experiences an uncertain threat,
it's no wonder that it has these effects on your behavior. Even
so, anxiety gives you an advantage by providing you with energy
and focus that can direct your attention. Since anxiety, like all
emotions, is non specific, when it is triggered you place it in the
content of your environment or current concerns (Schachter &
Singer, 1962). Anxiety has an undeserved bad reputation because
many people don't like the way it makes them feel, which may be
why some people seek ways to get rid of it rather than recognize
its benefits.

ANXIETY PROVIDES DIRECTION

The emotion of anxiety alerts you to pay attention to something,
but your interpretation of exactly what that may be is based upon
the attributions you make to your resulting feelings and thoughts. If
you are in a country where you do not understand the language and
ask someone for directions to a specific place, you might have a difficult time grasping the details beyond his hand signals. Such is the
language of emotion! The warning signs of anxiety—such as trem-
bling, twitching, sweating, dizziness, or a racing heart—can be helpful if you respond to them appropriately. For example, you might
be anxious in the morning because you have a big test that day. But
the nervous tension created by your anxiety can help remind you to
make sure you have everything you need, such as your calculator or
notes. So anxiety will give you a general direction by creating certain
uncomfortable feelings and thoughts; however, as with all emotions,
you have to decide what it is trying to tell you.

ANXIETY IS MOTIVATING

Neurological researchers believe that anxiety is fundamental to motivating your thoughts in ways that are beneficial and helpful (Luu, Tucker, & Derryberry, 1998). At optimal levels, the action potential of anxiety can sharpen your focus, help you to think on your feet, and energize you. Imagine how you might feel before a physical contest, such as running a race, where your nervous energy is invigorating and gives you a boost. The nervous energy provided by anxiety can be just as useful in situations that require using cognitive skills as it is in physical ones; that is, if you are otherwise prepared for the task.

Researchers have found that, for some students, added stress and tension—bodily responses to anxiety—improve creativity, productivity, and the quality of their work (Schraw, Wadkins, & Olafson, 2007). Suppose you have a paper to write. Are you likely to complete it ahead of schedule or at the last minute? An important attribute of successful people is that they are effective at meeting deadlines whether they complete their work ahead of the deadline or close to it, which is related to when their anxiety is triggered. Anxiety is activated in some people simply by the fact that they have a task to complete—they want to get it done so they don't have to think about it anymore. But for others, time pressure is necessary because a deadline triggers anxiety that provides energy and drive for them to complete a task such as writing a paper. People who prefer time pressure are often referred to as procrastinators, but this designation has come to have a derogatory meaning when in fact what's actually important is outcome—whether or not the person successfully completes tasks.

What makes some people who procrastinate successful in completing tasks and others fail at task completion? Researchers found that last-minute time pressure and the feeling of being challenged actually motivate procrastinators who are successful at task completion (Chu & Choi, 2005). These procrastinators were confident, preferred time pressure, and cognitively made a decision to procrastinate although they completed tasks by the deadline. The researchers distinguished between the two groups by referring to those who were successful in completing tasks by the deadline as "active" procrastinators and those who failed at task completion as "passive" procrastinators.

WHEN ANXIETY ISN'T A WELCOME FRIEND

Just like an unhealthy friend, your anxiety and how you read it might lead you astray, especially if you interpret the tension it creates as a need to eat junk food, use alcohol or substances, or do something harmful to yourself. But your response to anxiety is not the fault of the emotion, even though some people try to get rid of anxiety in unhealthy ways.

Some people will do nearly anything to avoid the feelings and thoughts that are created by the emotion of anxiety. People who have *anxiety sensitivity* are afraid of the bodily sensations of anxiety because they believe those sensations are a sign of an impending catastrophic event (Reiss & McNally, 1985). For example, they may interpret their rapid heartbeat caused by anxiety as a sign of an impending heart attack. Researchers found that anxiety sensitivity is linked to increased alcohol consumption and also risky drinking motives such as coping and conformity (DeMartini & Carey, 2011). However, this does not mean people will necessarily be inclined to use alcohol if they don't like how anxiety feels and what it makes them think. Whether alcohol use becomes a method of coping with anxiety sensitivity depends on other factors and motivations.

Your emotional system can lag with residual energy, much like a friend who lingers when you want him to leave. As it is with a friend who hangs around too long, you might become agitated, annoyed, or misinterpret what that emotion has signaled. What you might experience with focused anxiety can create bodily sensations that you interpret negatively because the cause isn't apparent or you have moved on. Anxiety is stimulating and it's no wonder that some people continuously drive themselves to get that rush. For example, you may have studied hard for a test and done well because your anxiety helped focus and energize you. Later, you might find yourself feeling antsy and agitated. But the lingering effect of anxiety that annoys you is the same friend who had helped create your earlier focus.

Although you may try your best to deal with anxiety when it is triggered, sometimes anxious feelings and thoughts are very difficult to manage, and this can lead you to worry about something in the present or future.

WHEN ANXIETY CREATES WORRY

You may be worried about an exam you have this week, or about attaining your career goals in the future. When you worry or have *repetitive thoughts*—thinking about the same thing over and over again—your mind is trying to make sense of anxiety that has been triggered. Worrisome thoughts about the future are a very handy target for your anxiety since your control over the future is limited. Although you may believe you are paying attention to whatever is making you anxious, worrying about the future that you cannot control could be a way to avoid thinking about what actually triggered your anxiety in the first place.

Usually worries are not pleasant because they lead you to consider a bad outcome, such as the possibility of something happening that you least desire, or the possibility of not reaching a goal. However, worries can be useful when they alert you to pay attention to behavior in the present that may affect your future, allow you to take a look at situations that require your focus, or inform you about what you can do in the present to make something possible in the future.

You might have become so worried about how you perform, appear, or behave that you have been accused of being a perfectionist. Perfectionism that is based on anxiety can be a useful trait, or it can interfere with your everyday life.

PERFECTIONISM

Perfectionism related to anxiety is expressed differently in people. For example, some people become concerned about doing something exactly right, and, as a result, have a tendency to change their minds several times before they are satisfied with an outcome. In contrast, others tend to require themselves to be exact in what they do. They may delay while thinking about how they might behave or complete a task, but when they actually perform it is with confidence and firm conviction. Perfectionism is not necessarily a bad thing. Healthy perfectionist behaviors might include striving for high standards that are achievable, or devoting your time to things you care about, identifying what works and what doesn't and how to make improvements (Szymanski, 2011). However, being a perfectionist to such a degree that it interferes with your health and well-being can represent anxiety that is disordered.

SUMMARY AND CONCLUSION

The emotion of anxiety is triggered when your brain experiences an uncertain threat. It creates arousal that you might experience in the form of nervous tension, excitement, restlessness, or difficulty with resting or sleeping. Anxiety may also lead you to be hyper-vigilant and thus you might become more watchful, alert, careful, or cautious.

Anxiety: What's It to You?

When you are having a difficult time managing anxiety, what can you do? The feelings that anxiety creates in your body at those times, such as restlessness, a rapid heartbeat, or sweating, can be distracting, especially when you have to stand in front of a group of people and give a presentation. However, it is important to push yourself past your anxiety by focusing on what you have to do. Taking a deep breath can help, and so can practicing and preparing beforehand as well as you possibly can. Also, it might help to get used to the unwelcome side of anxiety by continuing to do the kinds of things that make you feel uncomfortable.

When you are on alert as a result of an emotion that is triggered, you have to register, or be sensitive to, the conditions that will alleviate your anxiety following the task or project. For example, the lingering effects of anxiety could make it difficult to calm down, so you might have to plan a healthy way to calm yourself under those circumstances. Exercise is an excellent way to get rid of excess energy, or you may prefer to take a warm shower or bath in order to relax.

Anxiety can also be like a friend who keeps you awake when it's time to sleep. As the minutes tick by, your brain triggers anxiety that annoys you with reminders of things you must get done the following day. In such instances, it is important to identify what is important and what is not, what issues you can solve at the moment and what is better left for the following day. Before going to bed make certain that you are prepared for the next day in terms of reminders about what you need to do. Structure your environment to remind you by having a system that you can trust, such as putting everything you'll need for the next day in a certain place, or having a to-do list on your cell phone or on a notepad. Otherwise your friend, anxiety, might jolt you awake in order to help you to remember.

Yet anxiety also provides you with energy and focus that can direct your attention, and will give you a general direction by creating certain feelings and thoughts. Anxiety can result in worry about something in the present or future, and it may lead you to become perfectionistic. Perfectionism that is based on anxiety can be a useful trait, or it can interfere with your everyday life. The lingering effects of anxiety can disturb your sleep or keep you awake to remind you of what you have to do. Have a strategy in place so that your brain doesn't have to work overtime by triggering anxiety when it thinks you will forget something.

The differences between the emotions of anxiety and fear are complicated. Although there are many instances where you may want to welcome anxiety as an emotion that can help you achieve your goals, you may want to avoid a situation that activates fear. To understand the differences between anxiety and fear, read on to the next chapter that covers the complexity of fear.

CHAPTER 3

THE COMPLEXITY OF FEAR

As you are walking home alone, late at night, you hear the soft crackling sound of someone or something stepping on dry leaves nearby. Your heart begins to race as you imagine who or what lurks in the shadows. Should you run? Would it be better to stand still and listen?

Fear is generally considered a reaction to something immediate that threatens your security or safety, such as being startled by someone suddenly jumping out at you from behind a bush. The emotion of fear is felt as a sense of dread, alerting you to the possibility that your physical self might be harmed, which in turn motivates you to protect yourself.

From an evolutionary perspective, fear protected humans from predators and other threats to the survival of the species. So it is no wonder that certain dangers evoke that emotion, since fear helps protect you and is therefore adaptive, functional, and necessary. However, there is another important evolutionary aspect of emotions to consider that, in the case of fear, may be important to decision making as well as survival. Individuals who are *trait fearful*—those who tend to have personality characteristics that are dominated by the emotion of fear—will avoid taking risks that are generally perceived by others as relatively benign and prefer situations where such risks are absent (Sylvers et al., 2011). For example, in a study of risk taking, participants who were fearful consistently made judgments and choices that were relatively pessimistic and amplified their perception of risk in a given situation, in contrast to happy and angry participants who were more likely to disregard risk by making relatively optimistic judgments and choices (Lerner & Keltner, 2001). Thus, awareness of your emotions, and how they might influence your decision making in a given situation, is important in your approach to life, your work, and your goals.

FIGHT, FLIGHT, OR SOMETHING ELSE

The fear responses of *fight or flight* have been typically used to describe the behavior of various animals when they are threatened—either hanging around and fighting, or taking off in order to escape danger (Cannon, 1929). Yet it has also been recognized that animals and people have other responses to a threat. A person or animal might stand still or play dead and just "freeze" in response to being threatened, yell or scream as a fighting response rather than get physical, or separate from others as a flight response. As a result, some researchers suggest an expanded version of the fight-or-flight response, namely, "freeze, flight, fight, or fright" (Bracha, Ralston, Matsukawa, Matsunaga, Williams, & Bracha, 2004). Others have suggested that "tend-and-befriend" responses should also be considered, such as turning to others for help or social support, or making a situation less tense, dangerous, or uncomfortable in some way (Taylor, Klein, Lewis, Gruenewald, Gurung, & Updegraff, 2000).

The emotion of fear informs you to protect yourself in whatever manner would be most useful to you at that instant. With anxiety, you might imagine that something bad is going to happen; with fear, it is actually occurring. You may have encountered a situation in your life that led you to become intensely fearful at the time. People often recount stories of fear-producing encounters that have a good ending. But when you are in the midst of one, your brain and body are on high alert to seek a solution. What's most difficult is when you are trapped and the usual actions of fight, flight, or freeze are useless, and you are consequently filled with fright.

For example, consider what it might be like to be a passenger in a small aircraft and have the pilot anxiously inform you that the engine has failed. The terror you might experience would take the form of a rapid pulse, sweating, shortness of breath, and thoughts about dying. Although the pilot can still safely land, if there is a place in which to do so, the usual outlets to protect yourself are blocked and you must rely on the expertise of someone else to protect you. Even so, your fear will motivate you to find any way you can to protect yourself. Some people in such situations might pray or think positive thoughts for self-protection.

FEAR OR ANXIETY?

Both fear and anxiety are triggered in response to threat, so the differences between these two emotions can be confusing. Even in psychology literature you will frequently find the concepts used interchangeably. Fears of the unknown, a fear of death, contamination fear, a fear of flying, catastrophic fear, a fear of success, and a fear of failure are all commonly noted as a "fear" yet they are actually experienced as the emotion of anxiety. Similarly, phobias are considered to be an anxiety disorder (American Psychiatric Association, 2000), even though we think of a phobia in terms of something that is feared, such as insects, enclosed spaces, heights, or contamination. Yet fear and anxiety are important to differentiate, to the extent that one can do so. These emotions have been understood as keys to the dynamics of emotional illness because they can transform into behaviors that may lead you to avoid certain circumstances, or into ways in which you emotionally protect yourself that interfere with recognizing the reality of a situation (Ohman, 2010).

Some researchers distinguish between fear and anxiety by determining whether or not avoidance behaviors are present (Sylvers, Lilienfeld, & LaPrairie, 2011), or if the intended outcome has to do with avoidance or escape (Lang et al., 2000). The presence of avoidance behaviors would indicate fear, in contrast to anxiety where a person may be very much on the alert but does not avoid the situation. However, in certain anxiety disorders, such as phobias, the focus is specific and avoidance behaviors are present. How confusing! Perhaps a clearer distinction is that anxiety is foreboding and puts you on alert to a future threat, whereas fear immediately leads to an urge to defend yourself with escape from an impending disaster (Ohman, 2010).

FEAR AND TRAUMA

There are times when a past fear might re-emerge, even though the present situation does not truly warrant the need to be afraid. Such is the case of *posttraumatic stress disorder* (PTSD), where the consequence of a prior situation where you were in danger is emotionally re-lived in the present. Although you may intellectually know that you are safe, your brain automatically prepares you for the worst to happen—a situation that it recognizes has happened before—which speaks to the power of emotional memory in your brain's appraisal of a situation. A post-traumatic response can be triggered by a situation that is similar to a past trauma, the date on which a trauma occurred, a particular thought, or by a relationship that brings up an issue that is similar to a trauma that you have previously experienced. In a simple example, people who have been rear-ended in a motor vehicle accident frequently describe that for many weeks or months afterward they fear being rear-ended again and, as a result, find themselves vigilantly peering into their rear view mirror in anticipation of that happening.

Although a post-traumatic response may have to do with a situation in which fear was the primary emotion involved, PTSD is an anxiety disorder. The danger is not immediately present, but anticipated or expected based on a prior experience. So where the original trauma triggered fear, posttraumatic stress triggers anxiety that anticipates fear.

FEAR AND COMPETITION

Although fear can motivate you in some positive ways, researchers found that in competitive situations fear can interfere with success or get in your way if it causes you to change your strategy (Fernandez Slezak & Sigman, 2011). For example, when an opponent is stronger, you may be tempted to change from the typical strategy you might use when competing with someone who has skills similar to your own. Researchers testing this idea designed a study using a time-controlled chess game (Fernandez Slezak & Sigman, 2011). In the study, players whose opponents had weaker or similar skills played faster and their chances of winning increased. However, with stronger opponents, the players concentrated more on not losing, and they played more slowly, accurately, and cautiously. But in doing so their likelihood of winning decreased. In their attempt to avoid losing, the players had shifted their strategy to a more conservative approach that focused on preventing loss by being more cautious and playing slower and more accurately. Players increased the likelihood of winning against strong opponents when they adopted strategies they used against opponents with similar strength. So if you "fear" your opponent in a competitive situation, keep in mind that you may be more likely to win if you maintain your usual strategy rather than if you take on a more defensive approach.

Fear: What's It to You?

Is it best to push past the hesitation that holds you back or is it better to protect yourself? Imagine that you want to try surfing, but you are hesitant to take the risk because of your "fear" (which in this case is actually anxiety). The last time you tried to surf, when you were much younger, you became frightened by something in the water that could have been a shark. So should you try again? Such questions are difficult to answer when there is a threat of an actual danger, even if the threat is remote. Recognizing that it is perfectly acceptable to be afraid of some things, and complying with those fears, can be healthy if they do not interfere with your life in general. For example, you may be afraid of what's in the water, but you're not fearful of skydiving or snowboarding. But if you are afraid of every activity that takes you away from the safety of your home, you may want to seek help to move past some of these anxieties that are experienced as fears. Generally, it is normal and healthy to be afraid of some things, especially if you have had a previous experience that frightened you. If you decide to make an effort to overcome something that frightened you in the past, it might help to talk with others who are involved in the activity, research the subject to understand the probabilities of danger, and start slowly. However, if you decide that experiencing the emotion associated with the activity is just too unpleasant, figure out an alternative activity that you can do instead. And remember, if you weren't ever afraid then you would never protect yourself.

SUMMARY AND CONCLUSION

Fear is a reaction to something immediate that threatens your security or safety. It alerts you to the possibility that your physical self might be harmed, which in turn motivates you to protect yourself. There are various responses to threat taken by animals and people. The emotions of fear and anxiety are both triggered in response to threat; however, anxiety is foreboding, in contrast to fear, which immediately leads to an urge to defend yourself or escape. Posttraumatic stress disorder (PTSD) has to do with emotional memory, where you re-live in the present the consequence of a prior situation where you were in danger. In PTSD, the danger is anticipated based on a prior experience; thus where the original trauma triggered fear, a current and similar stress may trigger anxiety that anticipates fear. Individuals differ in trait fear; that is, how much their personality characteristics are dominated by the emotion of fear. Those who have high trait fear will avoid taking risks that are generally perceived by others as relatively benign.

You've likely encountered a situation where you were afraid you'd be embarrassed about something, although actually you were experiencing anxiety about the possibility of embarrassment. In any case, embarrassments happen all of the time, and perhaps a better understanding of them will help you the next time embarrassment is activated in you. The self-conscious emotion of embarrassment is the subject of the next chapter.

CHAPTER **4**

EMBARRASSMENT: BEING NOTICED WITH REGRET

Imagine sitting on a bench that happens to have drippings on it from someone's chocolate fudgesicle. You stand up and discover that the back of your light-colored pants has a chocolate stain right in the most unfortunate spot of all! For the rest of the day you must walk around with a chocolate stain, wondering if others think you couldn't make it to the restroom in time. You are embarrassed, which signals to others that you have violated a standard of behavior, even though what happened was not your fault. So, you find yourself explaining the chocolate stain and making elaborate stories about what happened to disown your embarrassment. Or maybe you just tie a sweater around your waist to cover up the stain. Even when it is no fault of your own, you can be embarrassed just based on how you think another person perceives you or the situation.

In most instances, being embarrassed happens when you do something accidentally, so it is unfortunate that you feel negatively about yourself when you had absolutely no intention of purposefully violating a social standard. According to researchers, most of the embarrassments that are encountered by people include instances of tripping and falling, spilling drinks, ripping their pants, stalling their cars, having one's private thoughts or feelings disclosed, accidental flatulence or belching, receiving undesired attention, and forgetting the names of others (Keltner & Buswell, 1996; Miller, 1992; Miller & Tangney, 1994; Sattler, 1966). It is likely that it would not take long for you to remember a unique embarrassing situation, since embarrassments are commonly experienced.

So what good is embarrassment if it makes you feel so uncomfortable? Our ability to be embarrassed likely serves to maintain social order, since in being embarrassed people communicate to others that they recognize and regret their misbehavior and will try to do better (Miller, 2007). The experience of embarrassment alerts you to your failure to behave according to certain social standards, which can be threatening to how you want others to evaluate you, as well as jeopardize the way in which you evaluate yourself. For example, if in the middle of giving an important presentation you inadvertently belch loudly, embarrassment would be linked to your concern that others, who generally hold a high evaluation of you, might instead critically judge you as you might judge yourself.

Along with guilt, shame, and pride, embarrassment is considered one of the self-conscious emotions. Given that embarrassment happens in relation to other people, it is a public emotion that makes you feel exposed, awkward, uncomfortable, and filled with regret for whatever your wrongdoing—accidental or intentional—happens to be. At the core of embarrassment and other self-conscious emotions is the potential for someone else to evaluate your actions, thoughts, and feelings negatively based on standards that govern our behavior (M. Lewis, 2008). For now, let's consider the ways in which embarrassment alerts others to how you feel.

SIGNALS OF EMBARRASSMENT

Human signals of embarrassment include a downward gaze, smile controls (such as a smile that is inhibited or one where only the corners of the lips turn upward), head movements that turn away, and face touching (Keltner & Buswell, 1997). Embarrassment has been linked to *social anxiety*—an intense experience of anxiety in social situations, particularly unfamiliar ones—because the signals of embarrassment and social anxiety are similar, such as the fear of negative evaluation and avoidance of eye contact (Leary & Kowalski, 1995).

However, there are vast differences in how people who are socially anxious process the facial expressions of others in contrast to those who are embarrassed. Where it was assumed that embarrassed individuals avoid eye contact, even though they were carefully attuned to how others regarded them, researchers have found instead that embarrassed individuals, unlike socially anxious people, look for emotional feedback from their audience in order to repair whatever damage was caused as a result of their social blunder (Darby & Harris, 2010). Thus, although embarrassed people may shift their gaze and glance down, they also seek cues about the emotional reactions of other people by looking at the expressions conveyed through the other person's eyes (Darby & Harris, 2010). So although we used to assume that an embarrassed person only looks away, now it is thought that they also glance at the other person's facial expression, particularly their eyes, for cues to help them decide what action they should take in order to repair the other person's perception of them, or just to see if their embarrassing behavior was noticed.

Another embarrassment signal is a blush. However, not everyone blushes upon being embarrassed. Blushing occurs when an emotional trigger causes your glands to release the hormone adrenaline in your body. Adrenaline has an effect on your nervous system, which in turn causes the capillaries that carry blood to your skin to widen. Since blood is brought closer to the surface of the skin, it causes you to blush. What's interesting about blushing is that receptors in the veins of human necks and cheeks dilate in response to social threat (Drummond & Lance, 1997). What's threatened in the case of embarrassment is one's social acceptance. However, blushing can be to your advantage because it is a distinct signal of sincere regret; blushing signals to others that you acknowledge your own mishap or social transgression and promotes trust and positive judgments by observers (Dijk, Koenig, Ketelaar, & de Jong, 2011). In other words, researchers have found that people who show embarrassment at their social transgressions are more prone to be liked, forgiven, and trusted than those who do not, and, as a result, their embarrassment saves face (Keltner & Anderson, 2000). So embarrassment does have a positive side, even if at the time you experience it you wish it never happened.

WHEN EMBARRASSMENT SEEMS TO PLAY BY DIFFERENT RULES

In specific situations and social circumstances, behavior that would ordinarily be considered embarrassing is embraced as amusing and humorous or disregarded as an embarrassment to the offender. For example, you may not be embarrassed to belch when in the company of a sibling, partner, or close friend. However, this same behavior would likely embarrass you while in the company of a stranger or someone who has a certain authority or status, such as an employer, a teacher, or the parents of your best friend. Thus, social context is taken into consideration by your brain when embarrassment is triggered.

In some circumstances your own pride or even a wish to be noticed can instead create embarrassment. Suppose, for example, that you are wearing something new that you hope others will think looks good on you. But if an observer points out the attractiveness of your appearance, you may experience embarrassment rather than pride. Thus, embarrassment can result from an experience where you become self-conscious and feel exposed, even if the situation has to do with something that is positive rather than negative.

WHEN THE EMBARRASSMENTS OF OTHERS AFFECT YOU

When a friend behaves in a socially inappropriate way, you may believe, as many people do, that your own reputation is going to be affected. Researchers studied six different situations in which observers rated people who were associated with someone whose behavior was publicly offensive—someone who burped loudly (Fortune & Newby-Clark, 2008). The people who were associated with the offensive friends most often felt that they would be judged in a negative way, along with the offending person. However, observers did not harshly judge the people who were associated with the offenders. So when a friend makes a big social mistake, don't think you will necessarily be judged along with them.

You may also be affected by a friend's unintentional embarrassing behavior, especially if you are prone to be embarrassed yourself. Participants in a study were given a chance to help another person by letting them know of a circumstance that might cause them embarrassment, such as having ink on their face when they were about to have an interview, or a situation where someone had a temporary flaw, such as food that was stuck in their teeth (Zoccola, Green, Karoutsos, Katona, & Sabina, 2011). Participants in the study who were more sensitive to embarrassment themselves were more hesitant to help others if their helping behavior might embarrass the other person.

If you are prone to embarrassment, you may want to give some thought to how you might feel if another person saved you from an embarrassing situation by nicely pointing out to you, for example, that you must have sat on some chocolate. Then decide if it is worth the risk of doing something similar for friends who might unknowingly embarrass themselves.

35

Embarrassment: What's It to You?

Think about something embarrassing that has happened to you. It's likely that you imagine everyone else became as preoccupied with that embarrassing situation as you were yourself. A phenomenon in social psychology known as the *spotlight effect* has to do with the fact that people overestimate the extent to which their appearance and actions are noticed by others (Gilovich, Medvec & Savitsky, 2000). People have a tendency to repeatedly replay an embarrassing event in their minds in which they were the main character.

Step back from your embarrassment and imagine how re-living the event over and over again in your mind can affect how you feel, the way in which you behave publicly, and your general mood. Likely it won't be good. Hanging on to your embarrassing mistakes can diminish your self-esteem and how you think of yourself generally. You are not your mistakes! Instead, your mistakes can help you to learn and grow. Granted, there are times when your friends want to remind you of the very amusing instance when you completely embarrassed yourself. Everyone dreads an embarrassment, including your friends, which is likely why they would prefer to focus on your social errors rather than their own. The honest response is to smile and admit that it was awful. Then let it go, remembering that people who show they are embarrassed by their social wrongdoing are most prone to be liked.

SUMMARY AND CONCLUSION

Most of the embarrassments that are encountered by people result from accidental behavior, and, as well, there are some positive circumstances where you might be embarrassed rather than experience pride. Embarrassment makes you feel exposed, awkward, uncomfortable, and filled with regret because it alerts you to your failure to behave according to certain social standards. People who are embarrassed seek signals regarding the emotional reactions of others by looking primarily at the expressions conveyed through their eyes. Embarrassment is associated with blushing; however, not everyone blushes upon being embarrassed. People who display embarrassment at their social transgressions are more prone to be liked, forgiven, and trusted than those who do not.

Embarrassments are awkward situations that you hope no one notices. Some emotion researchers have speculated that aspects of embarrassment are a less intense shame that is related to a negative self evaluation (M. Lewis, 2008; Tompkins, 1963). Although embarrassment and shame are possibly linked in some way, the behaviors associated with them involve distinct facial expressions and postures that separate them as emotions (M. Lewis, 2008). In any case, an embarrassment can be minor compared to shame, the subject of the following chapter.

CHAPTER 5

HIDING FROM SHAME

Shame is experienced as extreme self-consciousness that makes you want to hide. Yet there are people who hide their own shame by manipulating another person into experiencing it. This was the situation of Matthew, who secretly felt he wasn't good enough for his girlfriend and thought that she would leave him for someone else. He was insecure and felt inadequate for many other reasons, which were the actual sources of his shame. But since he was unable to deal with his feelings at the time, he found ways to strengthen his sense of security and adequacy which were, unfortunately, at his girlfriend's expense. By intentionally making his girlfriend jealous and self-conscious, she began to feel insecure and inadequate herself, and thus Matthew manipulated her into needing his approval. As a result, Matthew's girlfriend constantly felt inadequate and wanted to know what he was doing, thinking he was going to be with someone else who liked him, and wondered if she was attractive or smart enough for him. In a sense, Matthew gave away his own shame to her, which resulted in more confidence and security for himself.

Matthew's behavior is an example of how a person might try to rid himself of shame by imposing it on someone else, regardless of whether that person is a friend or adversary. Given how negatively shame is experienced, people will attempt to undo their state of shame in a number of ways. They may try to forget what caused their shame, reinterpret the situation or event in order to convince themselves that they are not shameful, or, like Matthew, place their own shameful feelings onto someone else (M. Lewis, 2008; Thomaes, Bushman, Stegge, & Olthof, 2008; Thomaes, Stegge, Olthof, Bushman, & Nezlek 2011).

Blaming or putting down others serves to disown what the shameful person feels. In order to escape shame's self-diminishing effects, a person might instead denigrate others or express contempt toward them. Thus a person might attempt to bolster his own view of himself by finding flaws in others so that they become the ones who are shameful. This is certainly true in the behavior of people who act like bullies. People who bully and tease can easily figure out what makes others ashamed, and they are highly skilled at triggering the emotion of shame in their peers. This makes shame a "contagious" emotion. Commonly, people believe that those who bully do so because they have low self-esteem. Instead, researchers have found that people who behave like bullies have high self-esteem, and that they are very *shame-prone*— fearing their failures or shortcomings will be exposed (Thomaes, Bushman, Stegge, & Olthof, 2008). Their mean behavior toward others keeps their self-esteem high because it takes their own and others' attention away from the parts of themselves about which they are ashamed. The shame that bullies hide is related to their tendency to experience hubristic pride, which will be discussed in Chapter 7.

What is it that makes shame such an uncomfortably powerful emotion that it might lead a person to work hard to get rid of it? Likely it's because shame is an emotion that seems to consume your entire self.

SHAME AND YOUR SENSE OF SELF

As a self-conscious emotion, shame informs you of an internal state of inadequacy, unworthiness, dishonor, or regret about which others may or may not be aware. In general, when shame is triggered, you feel bad about who you are—your whole self. Given that shame can lead you to feel as though your entire self is flawed or bad, it makes you want to hide or disappear (H. B. Lewis, 1971). Shame has a social purpose: the prospect of experiencing shame can keep you from behaving impulsively and doing something that might be considered socially inappropriate.

Shame is often confused with guilt—an emotion you might experience as a result of a wrongdoing about which you might feel remorseful and wish to make amends. Where you will likely have an urge to admit guilt, or talk with others about a situation that left you with guilty feelings, it is much less likely that you will broadcast your shame. In fact, you'll most likely conceal what you feel because shame does not make a distinction between an action and the self— what you've done as opposed to who you are (Lewis, 1971). Therefore, with shame, "bad" behavior is not separate from a "bad" self as it is with guilt.

Another person, circumstance, or situation can trigger shame in you, but so can a failure to meet your own ideals or standards. A situation, real or imagined, might trigger a shame response when you experience yourself to be inferior in a competition of any sort; when others might become aware of information that you want to cover up; or, if you anticipate being viewed as lacking or inadequate in certain qualities, such as in intellect, appearance, or performance. Your interpretation of a particular event or situation produces shame, more so than a specific situation or event itself (M. Lewis, 2008).

SHAME AND ANGER

Any situation that devalues the self and triggers shame can also trigger anger or even rage. This includes situations that stir up comparisons, evoke a fear of abandonment, or create fantasies about a rival's relative happiness, among other things. The anger experienced by a person who is shamed is like an all-consuming poison and it occupies a great deal of conscious thought.

Since shame is a painful and devastating emotion, theorists and clinicians have speculated that other forms of negative emotion, namely anger, are often expressed instead. Anger can allow a person to direct blame to something on the outside, and therefore hide any inferiority or exposure that is felt on the inside. Those who are especially vulnerable to shame may be more likely to hide their shame and become angry instead when they fail or are disregarded and ridiculed by others. Anger results in blaming something on the outside for causing a shameful event, such as having the thought that someone else did something to you, rather than blaming yourself and your own shortcomings for what happened. Investigators wanted to confirm if such shame-based angry responses do occur, especially among young adolescents—a time when people are quite vulnerable to shame (Thomaes, Stegge, Olthof, Bushman, & Nezlek, 2011). Their findings were consistent with notions that shame can trigger anger and hostility directed against others—a shame-based anger which they refer to as *humiliated fury* (Thomaes et al., 2011).

FEAR OF FAILURE

When you fear failure you wonder what other people might think of you or what you might think of yourself if you do not succeed in completing a project or in your efforts to realize a goal. An apprehension about failing can push you to accomplish something or it can lead to helplessness and shame. Thus, a fear of failure can activate and motivate you, or it can be crushing.

In order to use the fear of failure wisely, first it may be helpful to understand what the term actually means. The concept of fear of failure is unfortunately misnamed because the fear of failure has little to do with the emotion of fear—it is actually related to the emotions of anxiety and shame. Furthermore, the fear of failure is not about failure itself, but anxiety about experiencing shame that is associated with failing (Atkinson, 1957; Birney, Burdick, & Teevan, 1969; McGregor & Elliot, 2005). Even so, having a "fear of failure" simply sounds better than experiencing "anxiety about the possibility of shame." Thus, wanting to evade any humiliation that would accompany failure to achieve your goals, you may instead be driven to achieve. How interesting it is that apprehension about the possibility of experiencing an emotion motivates goal achievement for some people! But when you consider that shame is what's avoided in the fear of failure, the motivation to avoid it makes sense—shame is an emotion that people dread.

However, for some, the fear of failure may lead to giving up and embracing a familiar experience of shame. Quitting or withdrawing effort are also ways to protect oneself from the anxiety related to failure (Elliot & Thrash, 2004). Unfortunately, there are certain messages that you might convey to yourself when failure occurs. Failure can lead you to have a sense of unworthiness and an expectation that you will be abandoned emotionally or physically by others because you are not good enough (Elliot & Thrash, 2004). Thus, a fear of failure can be motivating and provide drive and focus toward a goal, or it can represent a painful state.

43

SHAME AS A MATTER OF CULTURAL PERSPECTIVE

Shame involves an evaluation of your sense of self, yet your sense of self is also impacted by the culture in which you live. The principles of Confucius in the Chinese culture distinguish between two concepts of self, namely the "big-me" and the "little-me," where the "big-me" represents a group, such as a family, society, or country, while the "little me," is first in the personal self as part of those groups (Zou & Wang, 2009). In Chinese society, people are expected to sacrifice their "little-me" in order to achieve the ideal morality level of their "big-me" (Zou & Wang, 2009). Although this concept is an intellectual one, researchers activated the "big-me" and "little-me" in people through an experiment (Zou & Wang, 2009). The researchers found that when individuals focus only on themselves, their "little-me," they are more likely to evaluate themselves harshly and experience shame with failure. In contrast, they are more likely to experience guilt rather than shame when they think their behaviors harm the groups that are part of their "big-me." According to the outcome of this study, how we feel, and not just how we think, plays a role in our perception of our self and the way in which we function in a society (Zou & Wang, 2009).

SUMMARY AND CONCLUSION

Shame is a self-conscious and social emotion that can lead you to feel as though your entire self is flawed or bad. A failure to meet your own ideals or standards can result in shame. In the experience of having a "fear of failure," in actuality it is not failure that is feared; rather, it is the shame associated with failing that people wish to avoid. A fear of failure can be motivating and provide drive and focus toward a goal or it can represent a painful state.

Shame: What's It to You?

Regardless of the trigger, when shame is experienced your perception of yourself suffers. In addition to the many emotions that can accompany shame, such as envy, anger, rage, and anxiety, we can also include sadness, depression, depletion, loneliness, and emptiness. And this is where shame can become a dangerous emotion. When shame is experienced as overwhelming, it can negatively color how you view yourself and how you assess the prospect of recovering your positive sense of yourself. Even so, people do recover from experiencing shame.

As with all emotions, shame requires perspective since it is placed in the context of one's environment and current concerns. Negative interpersonal experiences that activate intense emotions such as jealousy, envy, or anger can alert you to the possibility that shame is behind them. So you must guard against taking on shame that does not belong to you, and look at your potential to hide when the emotion of shame is triggered. Hiding often accompanies behaviors that are themselves a trigger for further shame, such as addictions, compulsive behaviors, or harsh self-criticism. When you are immersed in shame, attempt to move yourself out of it by considering the aspects of your life about which you have a sense of pride. If you have a hard time coming up with memories or current situations about which you are proud, consider what you have to do right now that will activate that emotion in you (see Chapter 7). Any improvement you can make in your life will ease you out of your shame.

Don't be afraid to accept responsibility for your own actions that have contributed to experiencing shame, and recognize when your own self-critical thoughts may activate that emotion. Remind yourself to always distinguish between being disappointed in your behavior and being ashamed of your entire self.

A person who feels shameful might instead denigrate others or express contempt toward them in order to escape shame's self-diminishing effects.

Shame is often confused with guilt—an emotion you might experience as a result of a wrongdoing about which you might feel remorseful and wish to make amends. In contrast to shame, the good news about guilt is that "bad" behavior is separate from a "bad" self. You can form your own opinion about whether or not it's good to have guilt as you read the next chapter.

CHAPTER 6

THE GOODNESS OF GUILT

Guilt is generally considered to be a social and self-conscious emotion that creates intense discomfort if your behavior—intentionally or unintentionally—hurts another person physically or emotionally. A positive side of guilt is that it motivates you to correct or repair whatever it was that led you to experience guilt in the first place. Thus, guilt is associated with actions and behaviors you can take to repair the failure (M. Lewis, 2008). Part of the motivation you will have to correct the situation is to relieve how guilt makes you feel and to restore the relationships you have with others.

Guilt alerts you to not behave in a way that might breech a social bond or a relationship in general. It is a social emotion because it informs you to have concern for others and to consider the other person's point of view. Your caregivers instilled in you a sense of right and wrong that also involved certain limits as far as behavior is concerned. As a result, going against what you consider to be the "right" behavior may trigger the emotion of guilt. Similarly, if you do something that leads you to evaluate your behavior as a failure, you will likely focus with regret and guilt on the actions that led you to fail (M. Lewis, 2008).

RESPONSES TO GUILT

People vary in their tendency or disposition to take action when they experience guilt. Some people readily make an effort to correct a situation where their actions led them to experience guilt, yet others seem to have a difficult time admitting a wrongdoing to themselves and taking corrective action. A person's response to the action potential of guilt can range from the inclination to apologize for nearly anything and experience guilt even for actions that are trivial to disregarding what most people would consider an extreme wrongdoing. Becoming preoccupied with doing the right thing can be just as hard on you as neglecting your standards. Being unable to recognize or own up to any wrongdoing makes correction nearly impossible. This is an area where guilt and shame interact, and knowing the differences may help you to better understand the various reactions of others when their guilt is activated.

GUILT AND SHAME

The differences between guilt and shame were studied in college students (Tangney, 1993, 1995). Shame experiences were rated as more painful and difficult to describe compared to experiences of guilt, and participants in the study said that shame made them feel physically smaller, more inferior, and powerless (Tangney, 1993, 1995). When compared to experiences of guilt, shame experiences were more likely to involve a sense of exposure and a desire to hide, and less likely to motivate confessing.

In contrast to shame, where the focus of failure is on your whole self, the focus for guilt is on behavior that caused the failure (H.B. Lewis, 1971). Yet some people experience shame when their guilt is exposed, so they might hide any wrongdoing. This can occur in everyday situations where, for example, someone catches you off guard and tells you about something you did that hurt his feelings. You may be inclined to apologize immediately. On the other hand, the confrontation itself may trigger the emotion of shame, which can make it difficult for you to offer an apology for correction.

SOURCES OF GUILT

Guilt is great at letting you know that you have hurt someone else. The possibility of correcting hurt feelings can relieve it, even if regret is not directly conveyed to the person who may be hurt. For example, Ron's father frequently lectured him about the importance of maintaining good grades. Ron knew that he could work harder at school, but at times he just wasn't motivated. When his father was hospitalized and had to undergo a serious surgery, Ron became understandably anxious but recognized that he mostly experienced guilt. He knew he was not responsible for his father's condition, but felt responsible that his father had worried about him. In an effort to relieve himself of guilt he promised himself that he would focus his attention on school.

Ron's situation is typical of guilt that young people might experience in relation to their parents, whether or not their circumstances are as extreme as Ron's happened to be. Researchers who studied descriptions of guilt-producing events in 5th, 8th, and 11th graders found that situations having to do with parents were a primary source of guilt at all grade levels (Williams & Bybee, 1994). In descriptions these researchers obtained, guilt feelings expressed by students more than doubled from the 5th to the 11th grades regarding situations involving neglect of responsibilities, inaction, and failure to attain ideals. Even though many students who don't feel they can live up to the expectations of their parents may instead express that they don't care, it is likely that they actually experience painful guilt.

As our society has changed, and the range of acceptable thoughts and behavior has increased, people do not necessarily experience guilt in situations where, in earlier times, guilt might have been triggered. Sigmund Freud (1930/1961a) believed that the primary sources of guilt were fear of authority and fear of loss of parental love, which eventually become one's *conscience*— an internal sense of right and wrong. Civilization, then, reinforces the sense of guilt and maintains order and stability. Over one hundred dred years ago, the practice of psychotherapy developed, to a large extent, because many people experienced intense guilt about their impulses and actions, which then caused them to develop symptoms. Treatment focused on helping patients attain the insight that their symptoms developed as a compromise between their wish to express an impulse and the prohibition against expressing it, such as guilt. At that time, and certainly up to a century later, many people had developed symptoms in response to intense guilt they felt about a thought, an action, or a wrongdoing.

Fortunately, it is not necessary to fear authority or the loss of parental love in order for guilt to be activated. The capacities to care for others, to care about the consequences of your actions, and to experience guilt are also related to empathy and pro-social behaviors that develop in response to early socialization experiences. This interpersonal approach to guilt, one that focuses on relationships, stresses that empathy and anxiety over loss of attachments are the two main origins of guilt (Baumeister, Stillwell, & Heatherton, 1994). Empathy is the ability to share the feelings, thoughts, or attitudes of someone else by recognizing the experience of another person and understanding what they feel. In this sense, guilt is triggered by experiencing empathic distress in response to the suffering of others combined with feeling responsible for the distress (Hoffman, 1982). In addition, anxiety that arises from the threat of being excluded socially or from alienating others with whom you have or want a relationship may take the form of guilt (Baumeister, Stillwell, & Heatherton, 1994; Jones & Kugler, 1993).

WHY BE GUILTY WHEN YOU'RE INNOCENT?

Suppose you are being blamed for something that is not your fault. Would you experience guilt? Since some people are prone to blame themselves for nearly everything that happens, as well as apologize for things that are not their wrongdoing, researchers Brian Parkinson and Sarah Illingworth (2009) wondered if guilt really is associated with higher self-blame in people. In their first study the researchers found that participants sometimes reported guilt when others close to them blamed them without good reason; however, this effect may have been due to their exposure to someone else's suffering rather than to their self-blame. They conducted a second study where participants were blamed for incidents when they were not the target of someone else's blame, and found that guilt ratings were lower. But for some of the participants simply being blamed led to reports of guilt. Given that there were situations in which people privately concluded that they are responsible for some negative event and felt guilty, the researchers conducted a third study that attempted to untangle the effects of self-blame and blame from others. Their third study confirmed that blame from someone else can lead to guilt, even when people don't blame themselves. The researchers concluded that since guilt can be activated even when you are not to blame, it may be that your guilt has to do with repairing the relationship more than it does with feeling personally to blame. In this case, the study confirms that guilt is a social emotion that helps you to maintain your relationships.

Guilt: What's It to You?

Guilt informs you to take action to correct a situation for which you bear some responsibility. You don't necessarily have to take action when the emotion of guilt is triggered. However, it might be wise to evaluate whether or not your guilt at the time is excessive, or what might be motivating you when you want to dismiss the message it is trying to convey.

Although guilt alerts you to a possible wrongdoing on your part, what you choose to do about it is up to you. For example, a girl who envies a peer might experience intense guilt about her own negative thoughts that have to do with hoping her peer fails socially. As a result of her guilt, she might be motivated to correct the situation by being complimentary or by promoting her peer to others. Whether or not there is something wrong with being nice when you are really envious and competitive might be controversial. But without the benefit of guilt, and the social standards and relationships that support it, the girl who envies her peer might instead humiliate her friend to everyone else on a social media site and have no concern about doing so. Depending upon your perspective, guilt may or may not be a good thing.

SUMMARY AND CONCLUSION

If your behavior intentionally or unintentionally hurts another person physically or emotionally, guilt will inform you to take action to correct the situation. In order to relieve how guilt makes you feel, you will be motivated to repair whatever it was that led you to experience guilt in the first place. People vary in their tendency or disposition to take action when they experience guilt. Some people can disregard their guilt when they harm others, or behave in ways that are self-centered. The range of acceptable thoughts and behavior has increased as our society has changed. People do not necessarily experience guilt in situations where, in earlier times, guilt might have been triggered. Early socialization experiences help to develop empathy and pro-social behaviors that are related to the capacities to care for others, to care about the consequences of your actions, and to experience guilt.

In addition to embarrassment, shame, and guilt, there is another self-conscious and social emotion: pride. Pride can provide you with enormous energy that helps you continue to pursue your goals.

CHAPTER 7

PRIDE AND HUBRIS ARE SELF-DEFINING

The primary purpose of emotions is to activate, direct, and motivate you towards a goal or an accomplishment. Even the emotion of pride has a purpose! Pride is a positive state that is associated with a specific action, and therefore people can activate this emotion and its subsequent positive state (M. Lewis, 2008). Finding ways to trigger pride in yourself may seem like an odd concept; however, it's likely an emotion that successful people attempt to create repeatedly. Pride can be like a healthy craving. And if you want an antidote to experiencing shame or embarrassment, find a way to activate the emotion of pride.

For example, Kelsey was embarrassed that she had felt so good about herself because the most popular guy in school had liked her—"had" being the defining word. Their relationship was over and getting past it seemed impossible when she felt so inadequate and humiliated. Kelsey had felt special being attached to Cody, but now she realized that it was just borrowed pride—she felt special because everyone adored him and he liked her. After a week of feeling awful about herself she began to recognize that she hadn't really liked herself enough even before her relationship with Cody. She wondered if feeling special is what she really missed the most, and she wanted that for herself. She was determined to find a way to feel good without him—to be proud of herself. If you were in Kelsey's shoes, how would you seek sources of pride?

WHAT YOUR PRIDE TELLS OTHERS

In social situations, the expression of pride tells others of your value, confidence, and importance. The non-verbal expression of pride—standing tall with chest extended, head tilted back, and a small smile—is recognized across cultures (Tracy & Robbins, 2007). You can likely imagine the difference in facial expression and posture when pride is felt in contrast to an emotion such as shame. Yet although the pride expression is universal, the acceptability of expressing this emotion varies among cultures.

The evolutionary purpose of the emotion of pride, it is assumed, was to convey one's social standing to others—an expression of pride would indicate that a person is important. High social status gave a person access to limited resources or a desirable mate, as well as other benefits. However, since we now live in modern society does that expression still work? Researchers Azim Shariff and Jessica Tracy (2009) wanted to find out if the expression of pride does, in fact, promote perception of high status. In six studies they found strong support for an association between the pride expression and the concept of high status when compared with other emotions such as disgust, fear, happiness, anger, shame, and embarrassment. In all six studies the association between pride and high status was large, suggesting that the pride expression—an expanded body posture, small smile, head tilted back, and arms extended—transmits an automatically interpreted message of high status. They concluded that pride sends a message to observers to seek out proud individuals as members of a social group, in contrast to someone expressing anger, where the person may appear to be powerful but the emotion signals threat and motivates avoidance in others. So, showing the pride you have in your achievements through your natural expressions can help you.

THE INTERACTION OF PRIDE WITH OTHER SELF-CONSCIOUS EMOTIONS

Given its involvement in self-evaluation and in the relationships you have with others, pride is considered a self-conscious emotion along with embarrassment, guilt, and shame. But where pride is felt as positive, embarrassment, guilt, and shame are associated with painful feelings. Yet these self-conscious emotions can interact, such as when you experience embarrassment, shame, or guilt in response to pride. For example, although you may gear your efforts toward accomplishments that will trigger pride, experiencing the emotion may subsequently trigger shame about your desire for recognition, guilt about leaving others behind, or embarrassment when others acknowledge your achievement. In addition, the emotion of pride can be triggered simply by refraining from an activity that would otherwise trigger embarrassment, shame, or guilt.

PRIDE AND MOTIVATION

When pride is activated it creates a positive view of yourself along with feelings of optimism and worthiness. Unlike self-esteem, which has more to do with a general attitude about one's own worth, pride is triggered in response to something specific, such as an accomplishment. Experiencing pride because of a success can lead you to imagine further and even larger achievements (Fredrickson & Branigan, 2001). Motivation to persevere in your attempts to achieve a long-term goal, or to sustain effort in a negative situation, can be aided by experiences that trigger the emotion of pride (Williams & DeSteno, 2008).

OVERCONFIDENCE FROM PRIDE

While pride in an achievement can instill you with confidence, it can potentially create an attitude that is overly confident. But is such overconfidence necessarily a bad thing? Actually, being overconfident can be helpful and, perhaps, even profitable. Although overconfidence can lead you to wrongly assess situations, have idealistic or unrealistic expectations, or possibly make risky decisions, it can also encourage you to compete, rather than retreat, in situations where you are capable of winning, and has positive effects on ambition, credibility, and morale (Johnson & Fowler, 2011).

We tend to believe people who are very confident, and, in fact, some researchers found that overconfidence is the best strategy when there is uncertainty about the strength of an opponent and the outcome, particularly in business (Johnson & Fowler, 2011). In such situations, where you have a chance of winning, the researchers surmised that the value of competing or fighting for something is worth the costs that are involved. Translated into evolutionary terms, for example, fighting for and subsequently winning a desirable mate may be worth the risk of getting injured. These researchers applied this concept more broadly to the use of deception in business, such as when the potential consequences that may result from false marketing or advertising are seen as worth the value of getting consumers to purchase a product. Such overconfidence, according to Johnson and Fowler (2011), assumes that the value of getting consumers to purchase products is worth the costs of competing in a deceptive way, and often disregards risks such as consumer disappointment, anger, or lawsuits; these risks in business are likely seen as less expensive than losing a competitive venture. So the next time you see a product falsely advertised, recognize that such a deceptive strategy to get you to buy it must seem worth the risks involved to those who are marketing the product.

HUBRISTIC PRIDE

Pride doesn't make you self-centered, but it can characterize hubris. Hubristic pride, which represents a more global and overly self-confident attitude, is related to being proud of who you are in an arrogant or egotistical sense (Tracy & Robbins, 2007a). Hubris generally translates into considering oneself as being highly valued. When you experience pride, you might consider that your actions resulted in something done well; with hubris, you feel you did something well because *you are great.* In a sense, hubristic pride does not separate the self from the deed (Lewis, 2008), much like the way the emotion of shame leads you to feel as though your whole self is bad due to an action on your part.

Researchers found that hubristic pride is related to *narcissistic self-aggrandizement*—enhancing or exaggerating who you are in a self-centered manner (Tracy & Robbins, 2007b). They also found that hubris is associated with shame-proneness and may be a way to hide feelings of shame, whereas individuals who tend to experience pride tend not to be shame-prone (Tracy & Robbins, 2007b). Emotions such as pride, hubris, and shame are complex and they can play starring roles in behavior. Chapter 5 discussed research indicating that people who bully have high self-esteem but are highly shame-prone. However, many people think of those who bully as having low self-esteem. We could speculate from the above research that the confidence of those who bully results from hubris. Thus they may have a hubristic pride—narcissistic self-aggrandizement—that hides their proneness to experience shame.

Since the evolutionary purpose of self-conscious and social emotions has to do with functioning within a group, pride indicates status to others and its expression can raise social standing. However, where pride can motivate behaviors that are geared toward the attainment of status, hubris falsely promotes it and may have evolved as an attempt to convince others of success even when it is unwarranted (Tracy & Robbins, 2007a). Likely you are aware of people who have falsely acquired social standing with confidence that isn't authentic, including people who are popular because they behave aggressively or like bullies. Nevertheless, hubristic pride is convincing and alluring, whether it's an attribute of someone who uses it to gain popularity or a trait of a self-important leader.

Pride: What's It to You?

The emotion of pride can help you to succeed. Pride builds on itself, and once you begin experiencing how it makes you feel and think, you'll want more of its effect. Pride creates confidence in achievements, in contrast to shame or guilt that can result from failure to achieve. However, it is important to have realistic goals that activate pride in your achievements along the way. Create small, achievable steps toward your ultimate goals. Rather than give up when you meet an obstacle, find a source of pride in your efforts, and another route if necessary. As you accomplish each step, pride motivates you to continue your efforts. Breaking down a goal to smaller steps that you can accomplish proudly may keep you from giving up because of experiencing shame or guilt due to failure.

Find a way to take a look at previous sources of pride when you are feeling down. Remind yourself of what you have accomplished and achieved, as well as the obstacles that you have overcome. Write a list of the things you want to do or what you would like to accomplish that would likely be sources of pride for you. Just having goals in mind can direct you. In the meantime, assume the posture of a person who is proud—stand tall with chest extended, head tilted back, and a small smile on your face.

SUMMARY AND CONCLUSION

Pride is a positive state that is triggered in response to a specific accomplishment—an achievement, an event, or a measure of performance. The expression of pride tells others of your value, confidence, and importance. Pride indicates status to others and its expression can raise social standing. Pride creates a positive view of yourself in addition to promoting optimism and worthiness. Although pride can potentially create an attitude that is overly confident, such confidence can be useful. Hubristic pride, which represents a more global and overly self-confident attitude, is related to being proud of who you are in an arrogant or egotistical sense. Hubristic pride does not separate yourself from the specific deed of which you are proud. Even so, in an evolutionary sense hubristic pride serves a purpose in terms of the information it conveys to others in a competitive situation.

Now let's turn to an emotion where isolation, either within or outside of oneself, is the focus. Loneliness will be the subject of the next chapter. It's hard to imagine that the emotion of loneliness serves a purpose; however, like other emotions, its activation provides you with information and motivation.

CHAPTER 8

LONELINESS HAS A PURPOSE

Jonathan had lived in the same house and had the same three close friends for ten years. Family circumstances made moving to another state necessary. Although he kept up with his friends by phone, email, and through social media sites, he missed having people to hang out with at school and on weekends. But even more than that, he missed having friends around who really knew him. For the first month in his new environment, Jonathan didn't want to go anywhere or do anything. He was tired, sad, and missed everything that was left behind, but especially his friends. When school began he met people who were friendly but it still did not seem that he would ever really get to know anyone. Even so, he tried. It took Jonathan nearly two years to feel he belonged in the new environment and could relate to the people around him, but he did make good friends once he learned not to compare how he felt about them to the friends he had left. He anticipated having to start all over again when he went to college, and by then he knew very well that acquaintances take time to develop into lasting friendships.

When you're lonely, it's unlikely you'll remember that emotions serve a purpose, since what possible purpose can the heartache of loneliness serve? If you think about how this emotion makes you feel and think, then, like Jonathan, you will recognize that it alerts you to the fact that your relationships do not satisfy your need to belong. Beyond that, loneliness is designed to motivate you to take necessary action to relieve it, although what you decide to do when you experience a certain emotion is up to you. Loneliness is sometimes mistaken for a depressed mood—a state of sadness, disinterest in activities, and difficulty with engaging in life, among many other symptoms—since there may be periods of time when a lonely person feels helpless to make a difference in the situation.

You can be lonely whether or not you have a romantic relationship, relatives, or many friends. When you have a need and desire to be interpersonally connected and recognize that it's missing, you may become wrapped up in the emotion of loneliness. Emotions, by definition, are immediately felt when triggered by a particular event or stimulus. Loneliness can be triggered when you're thinking of a significant relationship that has ended, if you realize that your relationships are not emotionally satisfying, if you have lost a loved one, if your access to social relationships has changed because of a life circumstance, or at the moment you recognize that you are not truly known and understood by another.

In an attempt to better understand the common features or properties of a person who is lonely, psychological researchers developed a profile of the major feelings, thoughts, and behaviors of a lonely person (Horowitz, French, & Anderson, 1982). These features, which were almost exclusively interpersonal, included: isolation of self from others, feeling not liked by others, feeling excluded from other activities, feeling inferior, and believing one does not know how to make friends. Other researchers found that loneliness is related to certain personal characteristics, which included shyness, low self-esteem, feelings of alienation, belief that the world is not a fair place, and having an external locus of control—a belief that others, fate, or chance determine events and decisions in your life, and not yourself (Jones, Freemon, & Goswick, 1981).

Common themes in the traits of the prototypical lonely person seem to be feelings of low self-worth and a sense of helplessness. If this is the case, then a lonely person may not approach a potential relationship in an appealing way or with effective social skills. Some researchers have pointed out that, unfortunately, loneliness can be maintained because the lonely person is hyper-alert and, as a result, is oversensitive to possible rejecting behavior of others (Weiss, 1973). The lonely person's expectations regarding friendships may be exaggerated and, as a result, others do not measure up (Jones et al., 1981). In addition, others may see a lonely person's hesitation as aloofness or as disinterest in social involvement (Jones et al., 1981).

Loneliness can make you feel empty and long for someone to really know you. If you are without friends, you may wish to have someone in your life who will relieve your feelings of emptiness. Yet loneliness may not be clearly linked to the reality of a situation because it can exist despite numerous friendships you might have, since connections with others may be fleeting, meaningless, or not what you consider to be significant. Thus, you can have many friends, or be in a room filled with people, and still be lonely.

RECOVERING FROM LONELINESS

People have a need to be connected with others, and, although this may sound odd, your brain may try to help you to find friends. Researchers studied people who were recently excluded from relationships and found that these people may behave in certain ways in social situations just because they need that connection (DeWall, Maner, & Rouby, 2009). Excluded people in that research study paid closer attention to others who had smiling faces, as opposed to those whose faces showed disapproval, thereby seeking emotional contact and attempting to find others who are accepting. The researchers concluded that people who feel the threat of social exclusion are highly motivated to look for sources of acceptance, and their perceptions are in gear to find a friendly face (DeWall et al., 2009). Their study illustrated that being connected to others is important, and it shows in the basic ways in which you humans have evolved to seek out others.

If you are lonely you may wish that someone would just come along and be a friend to you. But a much faster way to end loneliness is for you to take the first step. Self-disclosure, taking risks socially, being assertive, and being responsive to others are useful strategies to defeat loneliness (Davis & Franzoi, 1986). Since loneliness can lead to self-absorption and a high sensitivity where you look to others for positive affirmation, it is important to remain mindful of the needs of others in social interactions, as suggested by researchers Mark Davis and Stephan Franzoi (1986), who studied adolescent loneliness and self-disclosure. These researchers suggest that talking about yourself and listening to another person's response to what you've said can help to reduce feelings of loneliness.

ALONENESS AND LONELINESS

Aloneness is different than loneliness. Although the two are a bit conflated, you can feel either without the other. The amount of time you spend alone has little to do with being lonely. Many people find solitude to be a pleasant experience that allows them to think, be creative, rest, or simply pass time in solitary activity. There are people in whom fear or anxiety is triggered when they are alone, but this is different than the experience of loneliness, as are situations where a person prefers to be alone in order to avoid the anxiety that can come along with social activities.

LONELY MOODS

A lonely mood is like a lingering sadness, but with a particular referent; it's sadness about not having someone in your life with whom caring and deep understanding is mutually felt. Emotions differ from the prolonged emotional states that define moods. Even so, a prolonged loneliness can lead you to believe that you are depressed, even though depression differs from loneliness in a number of ways. People who are lonely are more likely to focus on their lack of relationships for how they feel than are people who are depressed (Anderson, Horowitz, & French, 1983). However, both lonely and depressed people may have a tendency to blame themselves or their abilities for their failure to have satisfying relationships with others (Anderson et al., 1983).

THE NEED TO BELONG

Across cultures, humans are motivated by a need to belong, and their emotions and behaviors are geared toward satisfying this need (Baumeister & Leary, 1995). Far more effort gets put into maintaining social bonds than dissolving them. Although you can't get rid of lonely feelings with simple personal contact that is inconsequential, personal contact is an important step in the process of making a lasting connection with another person.

Studies of college students have found that people who are less lonely have a greater willingness to talk about themselves and what they feel, and they experience greater closeness to others when they do reveal things about themselves (Davis & Franzoi, 1986). So it appears that an opportunity to have someone else get to know you by talking about yourself makes you feel closer to another person and less lonely.

Loneliness: What's It to You?

Loneliness, like all emotions, creates certain cognitions and therefore can cause you to imagine that everyone else has the kinds of affiliations that you strongly desire, or that other people are enjoying the company of others while you are feeling inadequately connected. Your longing for closeness may, at times, lead you to believe that your situation might never end. It's understandable why people who are lonely might feel unwanted, unknown, undesirable, insignificant, despairing, insecure, or abandoned. Being connected to others makes one feel valued, and when you experience the emotion of loneliness you will try to make sense of it, even if you blame yourself in the process. Blaming yourself may be a simple context in which to place your lonely feelings, but converting those thoughts to what you can do differently might help you find a way out of your lonely state.

Being willing to talk about yourself and to have interactions where you discuss personal information with peers—who you like, something silly you did, or even what subjects in school are difficult for you—was associated with being less lonely. This means that you should say something about yourself to that person sitting next to you or standing in line with you. Yes, it is taking a risk, but if you want to be less lonely you are better off not waiting until someone comes along and connects with you.

Although it seems logical that you have to find someone you believe you can trust in order to share personal information, it is possible that sharing personal information with another person can also lead you to trust that person more and experience closeness that can rid you of loneliness. In addition, researchers have found that a warm and supportive relationship with family members, even one that does not necessarily involve self-disclosure, can help with feelings of loneliness (Davis & Franzoi, 1986).

SUMMARY AND CONCLUSION

Loneliness alerts you to the fact that your relationships do not satisfy your need to belong, and it can be experienced even when you have a romantic relationship, relatives, or many friends. As a result, loneliness motivates you to take necessary action that will relieve it.

Feelings of low self-worth and a sense of helplessness are commonly experienced by lonely people. Aloneness is different than loneliness, and you can feel either without the other. People have different needs for solitude or passing time in solitary activity. A prolonged loneliness can lead you to believe that you are depressed, even though depression differs from loneliness. Personal and meaningful contact is an important step in the process of making a lasting connection with another person.

When you are lonely you may find yourself hoping for some one to come along with whom you can share activities or personal reflections. You may want to learn more about the complex experience of being hopeful. Hope is the subject of the next chapter.

CHAPTER **9**

HOPE AND RECOGNIZING WHEN IT'S HOPELESS

Tyler wanted to attend a concert featuring his favorite band, knowing that Emma, whom he was very interested in dating, would be thrilled to see this band as well. But the tickets had sold out. A friend texted him saying that she heard someone might have two tickets for sale, and thus he was hopeful that he could get tickets (and a date with Emma). His thoughts turned to the future possibility of going to the concert with Emma and his mood changed for the better. He grabbed his phone to call her, completely ignoring any possibility of later disappointment if the tickets weren't available.

Similar to wishing and optimism, hope creates a positive mood about an expectation, a goal, or a future situation. Such mental time travel influences your state of mind and alters your present behavior and how you feel. The action potential of hope can lead you to believe so much in a future possibility that, like Tyler, you may not fully consider probabilities.

Controversy exists as to whether or not hope is an actual emotion or better understood as a thought that creates a certain mood—a prolonged affective state—lacking the immediacy and intensity of reflexive emotions yet capable of determining one's outlook on life. However, similar to emotional experiences generally, the activation of hope from a specific event can create a physiological and cognitive response that results in a positive feeling of expectation. The emotional basis of hope is also indicated in its ability to motivate behavior by spurring efforts to improve a situation while keeping you focused on the outcome you desire, in its effect on your judgment and decision making, and in helping you to act on your own behalf (Averill, 1994; Bruininks & Malle, 2005; Lazarus, 1999).

THEMES OF HOPE

There are many diverse situations in which hoping for a good outcome becomes a part of your thinking. You might hope to be successful in a competition, hope for the recovery of someone who is ill, or, like Tyler, hope for concert tickets in addition to the possibility of starting a romantic relationship. Actually, hoping for a romantic relationship, when you are not involved in one, may have real utility as far as well-being is concerned. Falling in love buffers you against certain physiological reactions to stress and can promote health (Schneiderman, Zilberstein-Kra, Leckman, & Feldman, 2011). It is possible that hoping for a relationship leads people to seek one for their own well-being, and this may be part of our biological make-up.

HOPING, WISHING, AND OPTIMISM

Hope is associated with wishing and wanting something positive to happen. However, in contrast to a wish, some believe that hope involves an expectation of the situation to occur in spite of the odds, as though hoping for something to happen involves the idea that it is less likely to occur than does wishing that it will (Bruininks & Malle, 2005). Another state that is similar to hope is optimism, and these concepts are often used interchangeably. However, one difference is that with hope there is a specific context and expected outcome—you are hoping for something specific to occur—but optimism is a more general attitude (Averill, 1994; Bruininks & Malle, 2005) Optimism is regarded as a more confident expectation of a certain outcome than hope since with hope the possibility exists of a negative outcome as well (Lazarus, 1999).

HOPE AND THE PLACEBO EFFECT

Given that hope is associated with specific outcomes, we might wonder if in certain situations having hope can actually influence what happens, or at least how we perceive an outcome. For example, if you are hopeful, based on a store clerk's testimony, that a certain nutritional supplement will give you more energy, how much of any effect can you attribute to the supplement and what part of the effect is simply related to your hope? Such questions arise in studies that have been conducted regarding medications. In order to distinguish the physical effects of a medication from other psychological, social, and neurobiological factors, clinical drug trials compare a medication with an inactive substance, commonly referred to as a placebo.

Some studies of antidepressants showed effects similar to a placebo especially when the placebo is engineered to produce side effects, causing those who take it to believe that they are on the actual medication (Benedetti, Mayberg, Wager, Stohler, & Zubieta, 2005). This does not necessarily mean that such medications do not help people who are depressed, but it is possible that factors related to personality and disposition, such as optimism or hope, may contribute to improved mood. For example, specific activity in brain regions of those who had high expectations of improvement, whether on the actual drug or the placebo, was different than those who did not have expectations (Benedetti et al., 2005). Placebo effects are complex, and studies are attempting to find psychological and neurobiological explanations, including the power of hope.

HOPE AND THINKING

Yet even with the doubt that lingers, along with hope comes your prediction that you will be happy. The positive feelings you experience as you look ahead, imagining hopefully what might happen, what you will attain, or who you are going to be, can change how you currently view yourself. Hope also helps you get past obstacles to reach a specific goal. The way in which you think when you are hopeful can provide motivation to pursue your goals and creative ideas that may help you solve problems.

Hope can change your thinking, but can having hope also help you to think? Positive emotions have been associated with problem solving and flexibility in thinking. Many people believe that there are optimal times during the day in which they think most clearly, or are most creative and imaginative. So can hope help you during those times that are least optimal for you? Since hope can make people strive toward positive outcomes, researchers wondered if eliciting hope in participants could affect their functioning (Cavanaugh, Cutright, Luce, & Bettman, 2011). The researchers chose the time of day that was not the best for the participants in terms of their being able to think most clearly and be most creative and imaginative. Their findings demonstrated that hope helps people to perform better on certain intelligence tasks, and it increases imagination and mental exploration during times of day when people are not their best in terms of being able to think clearly. The researchers concluded that positive emotions can motivate certain behaviors and help a person to use their skills. Therefore, it might help to think positively and be hopeful when your energy is low and it's not your best time of day to think or be imaginative. Being hopeful and positive can give you some of the energy you might need to focus and complete a task. So think about the great grade you'll get on the paper you have to write or, before you start writing, take a moment and imagine something fun that you're going to do on the weekend.

GIVING UP HOPE

There are times when accepting reality means you must give up having hope. When you consider what might have been, in contrast to what exists in the present, you may experience disappointment— the experience of sadness involving unfulfilled hope. Sometimes people seem to twist their thinking in an effort not to recognize a true disappointment. Perhaps one of the reasons one might avoid acknowledging disappointment is because it represents a finality— the recognition that you don't have, didn't get, or will never achieve whatever it is that you wanted. You might instead become angry with someone, which could be easier to experience than your disappointment. Disappointment forces you to admit that you do not have what you wish, and so it may be easier to protest with anger than it is to encounter your sadness about the course of events. In an obstinate way, anger will allow you to continue hoping for what you believe could have been. Disappointment, however, accepts reality.

In relationships, sometimes abandoning hope is psychologically healthier than holding onto it. Disappointment has commonalities with loneliness, separation, and loss, especially as it concerns a friend-ship or love relationship (Izard, 1991). Relinquishing hope is hard to do, because it means that you have failed to get what you expected from your relationship.

Giving up hope can also be very constructive and positive in situations where turning your attention elsewhere is necessary in order to actually reach your goal. So if you are determined to pursue a goal, but you encounter many roadblocks, you should consider if the approach you are taking is the best, and if there are other ways in which to achieve your objectives that perhaps you have not noticed. In our culture there is a particular glamour attributed to those who persist and win, in spite of limited hope for success. At the same time, having the strength to recognize when hope should be relinquished, and the courage to acknowledge your helplessness, can point you in a direction that is accompanied by new hope.

Hope: What's It to You?

Since having hope is to imagine that something positive will happen, many motivational principles direct people to visualize what they want and imagine positive outcomes so that their behavior is unconsciously structured to create them. However, since most of the things we do are unconsciously processed, there are simple ways to make use of the positive effects of hope. Thus, consider your goals or your endeavors before bedtime, or even go over your to-do list. This is worthwhile since your brain is sensitive to your conscious perception of future events and will unconsciously work toward your goals. You may be a person who does not express hope when it is activated, and tell yourself that you don't want to have hope for something because acknowledging that you have hope also creates the possibility of being disappointed. Yet if hope is triggered you will, at least, secretly experience it and the good feelings it creates. Hopefully you won't take those good feelings away from yourself so quickly with the notion that you must protect yourself from disappointment. Instead, attempt to have a different relationship with disappointment so that you are not afraid of it. Finding ways to be resilient when things don't turn out as you had hoped can better protect you. These strategies may include, for example, thinking about what you learned from the situation and how that learning can be applied to future experiences; making a new plan for something that is achievable and considering what you will do to reach your new goal; separating your view of yourself from the outcome of an event by continuing to have a positive view of yourself regardless of the outcome; and finding ways to improve yourself that will trigger pride in you.

SUMMARY AND CONCLUSION

Hope creates a positive mood about an expectation, a goal, or a future situation. Controversy exists as to whether or not hope is an actual emotion or better understood as a thought that creates a certain mood. However, as with emotions, the activation of hope as a result of a specific event creates a physiological and cognitive response. The way in which you think when you are hopeful can provide the motivation to pursue your goals and creative ideas that may help you to solve problems. Thus, hope can affect your judgment, decision making, and self-interest. Hope is associated with wishing and optimism. Although these concepts differ, they are often used interchangeably.

There are times when accepting reality means you must give up having hope. Disappointment is the experience of sadness involving unfulfilled hopes, but giving up hope may help you to turn your attention elsewhere in order to reach your goal. Even so, sadness can be a difficult emotion to experience, especially when it involves grief or a relationship that has dissolved. Perhaps an understanding of sadness, which is covered in the next chapter, can help you to recognize its benefits the next time you are sad.

CHAPTER 10

SADNESS AND SAD LOVE

Luis had a very strong bond with his dog, Hawk, who was part of the family for ten years. Hawk slept next to Luis' bed, and both Luis and his father were responsible for Hawk's care. The illness that took Hawk's life was devastating to the family, and especially to Luis and his father. When friends who were unaware of the loss visited and asked about Hawk, Luis told them the facts about the illness, but said nothing about his sadness. During the night Luis' sadness made him stir, and for weeks he would wake up in the middle of the night fully expecting to find Hawk at the foot of his bed. However, Luis had a difficult time letting anyone know about his own sadness, even though it likely showed on his face. Eventually, when he began worrying about still being sad, Luis told his counselor about Hawk, his worry that he was not supposed to be so sad, and how he couldn't seem to get over losing him. His counselor advised Luis to do some things to remember Hawk and share with others—making a collage of photographs, writing poetry about Hawk, and making a list of what Luis loved most about his dog—rather than keep trying to forget his sadness.

Sadness is a painful emotion of disconnection from someone or something that you value or had valued. Sadness helps you to remember, rather than forget, what it is or was that you desired. In doing so, it promotes personal reflection following a loss that is important to you, and turns your attention inward in a way that can promote resignation and acceptance (Izard, 1977; Lazarus, 1991). Thus, the emotion of sadness attempts to assist you by giving you an opportunity to consider the impact of your loss and the necessity of revising your objectives and strategies for the future.

When sadness is triggered, a heavy wistfulness or longing is felt. Your brain has determined that you have experienced a disappointment or a lasting loss. Sadness alerts you to acknowledge a loss that you might otherwise wish you could deny. The facial expression associated with sadness signals a need for comfort and makes others aware of your need (Ekman, 2003).

Sadness impacts how you perceive others and yourself. One study found that sadness tends to decrease your confidence in first impressions (Schwarz, 1990). Another found that the experience of sadness leads you to struggle with the painful, existential question, "Who am I?" (Henretty, Levitt, & Mathews, 2008).

The tired feelings that come with sadness can lead you to assume that you can't think clearly or muster up the energy to get things done. However, according to a research study, sadness or a sad mood does not affect cognitive processes such as attention, memory, problem solving, verbal reasoning, or the ability to be mentally flexible and multi-task (Chepenik, Cornew, & Farah, 2007). However, the results of the study indicated that sadness or a sad mood did affect the accuracy of identifying facial expressions of emotion, and the ability to recall emotion-related words. So if you are experiencing sadness, it might be best to distract your brain with a task that is not related to your emotions.

SADNESS AND DEPRESSION

The emotion of sadness is not the same as a state of depression, although many people use these words interchangeably. Sadness and depression differ in several ways, although both may be the result of loss (Izard, 1991). Depression is longer lasting and can involve other emotions such as guilt, shame, or anger. What causes a state of depression may be uncertain, whereas sadness is an emotion that is clearly triggered in response to someone or something. The biological, genetic, psychological, and socio-cultural theories regarding depression are numerous. But where sadness is a natural and normal emotion to experience, depression occurs when your emotions are disordered.

SADNESS AND GRIEF

Sadness differs in terms of quality and duration from grief. Grief may be a result of the loss of a loved one or the result of a life circumstance. It is longer lasting than sadness, and may have a greater impact than sadness on your perception of the world. Emotions, such as sadness and agony, are very much involved in the experience of grieving; however, grief is not considered to be an emotion but rather a process of coping with loss (Lazarus, 1999). When sadness is experienced there is resignation and hopelessness about a loss; however, the experience of agony about a loss expresses protest (Ekman, 2003).

Mourning describes the emotional process in which you gradually adapt to a loss. There have been many theories about the course of mourning. Early in the last century, Freud (1917/1961b) speculated that in order to recover from loss, the person had to slowly withdraw emotional ties to the person they loved and reinvest their energy into others. Freud's belief that grieving should be limited in time was accepted and formed the basis of many theories about bereavement that followed. Although he emphasized that people must work through a loss, Freud also understood that grieving over the loss of a loved one could continue throughout one's own life.

Later in the last century, John Bowlby (1963), who developed theories concerning attachment, noted that certain behaviors, such as crying, clinging, and searching, are typically a child's responses to loss, and that there are parallel behaviors among adults who are in the midst of grieving. Such behaviors, according to Bowlby, are an attempt to reconnect with the loved person and also serve the purpose of gaining the care, support, and protection of others.

The notion that the process of grieving has stages is primarily based on the conceptualization of Elisabeth Kübler-Ross (1969) that originally had to do with the stages a dying person experiences. These stages include denial, anger, bargaining, depression, and acceptance. In terms of grieving, the stages involve an initial shock, acceptance of the reality of loss, working through to the pain of grief, adjustment to the environment without the person, emotional acceptance of the loss and moving on with life, and rebuilding faith that is challenged by the loss. Kübler-Ross believed that an outcome of going through these stages is regaining emotional and psychological health.

Unfortunately, stage theories, such as the one based on the work of Kübler-Ross, do not take into account how emotional memories—appraisal tendencies that may be activated—can later create the feelings that were originally associated with loss. As a result, when sadness about a loss was later activated, some people were erroneously prone to think it was because they had not adequately worked through the stages of mourning. Contemporary ideas regarding mourning and grief-related sadness question whether people go through stages in the process of grieving. Instead, they assume that various cognitive, environmental, relational, and emotional factors affect the grieving process, and acknowledge that emotional memories are powerful reminders of loss (Archer, 2001; Bonanno & Kaltman, 1999).

Emotions regarding a loss can be triggered throughout one's life and continue to cause sadness, although the feelings may not interfere with everyday functioning. Sometimes they are activated due to anniversary reactions, such as the birthday or death day of the lost loved one, or any significant holiday in which you might want to be with that person. Emotions related to grief can also be triggered by an age-matching anniversary reaction, when your age matches the age at death of a caregiver. Reminders, such as visiting a place you've been with that person, can also activate sadness. As time passes, the intensity of feelings about a loss will lessen as experiences in your life, including your relationships with others, create new memories. Even so, the memory of your loss remains in the background of your mind and can be triggered whenever there is a situation that makes you think about the lost loved one.

Thus, you don't necessarily "get over" a loss since you cannot voluntarily erase emotional memories. Instead, you must figure out what you are going to do when your emotional memories are activated. Emotions associated with grief inform you to remember. You can remember what you learned from the person you lost, remember what you enjoyed, and you can cry from recalling what you miss about the lost loved one. Even if your grief is about a relationship that has dissolved, there is always something that you may want to consider when your emotional memories stir up an old grief response.

Losing a pet is like losing a member of the family. This was certainly felt by Luis, whose experience of the loss of his dog, Hawk, began this chapter. A research study stressed the importance of sharing the feelings you have in response to the loss of a pet, which some people tend to ignore compared to the loss of a human loved one (Brown, Richards, & Wilson, 1996). Yet pet loss can be profound, especially because the relationship you have with a pet can be one that is intensely close, dependent, and unconditionally loving.

SAD LOVE

Profound sadness as it relates to love can be triggered by an observation, an event, a remembrance that your love is unrequited, or an acknowledgement that the object of your affection is inaccessible. Researchers who had studied the concept of love among people in the United States, Italy, and China found that it has both similar and different meanings across cultures, including the presence of love-related concepts among Chinese people such as "sad love," "sorrow-love," and "tenderness-pity" (Rothbaum & Tsang, 2004).

The concept of sad love seems as indefinable as love itself, although most people understand exactly how sad love feels. There is often sadness, and sometimes grief, when romantic relationships end. Love adds intensity and complexity to sadness, where the desire experienced with love becomes flavored by the dejection and helplessness felt with sadness.

Love does not technically meet the criteria of an emotion, and can be described instead as an emotional state or a mood. However, love has been considered also as a mixture or pattern of emotions that includes excitement, joy, happiness, or sensory pleasure (Izard, 1977). So if we are going to be picky about what constitutes an emotion, then love may not qualify. However, the concept of sad love seems to capture profoundly and succinctly the emotional impact of love that has gone sadly.

Sadness: What's It to You?

Nobody likes to be sad, as evidenced by all the things people do in order to avoid it. Some people potentially hurt themselves with medication, alcohol, drugs, food, sexual behaviors, and risky activities in an attempt to avoid or to relieve sadness. Yet, if sadness can help you to remember and accept reality, achieve insight that can realign your goals, alert you to be cautious before making decisions, and create an opportunity for you to slow down and observe yourself, then perhaps its adaptive purpose is evident. Like all emotions, sadness, in spite of how it makes you feel, is simply trying to protect you.

Talking about your sadness with someone you trust can help you feel less alone with it, and help you to be connected with other people, which can relieve your sense of loss. If you are sad because you have lost someone you love, it is important to pay attention to those times when your emotional memories are activated, such as the birthday or anniversary of the loss of that person. Thinking about your sadness during those times, rather than trying to push it aside, will help you get through what you feel and move on again.

SUMMARY AND CONCLUSION

Sadness is activated when you experience a disappointment or a lasting loss. Sadness turns your attention inward as you recognize a disconnection from someone or something that you value. The emotion of sadness is not the same as a state of depression, although many people use these words interchangeably. But where sadness is a natural and normal emotion to experience, depression occurs when your emotions are disordered. Grief, the loss of a loved one or the result of a life circumstance, differs from sadness in terms of quality and duration. You don't necessarily "get over" grief since you cannot voluntarily erase emotional memories. It's important to figure out what you are going to do when your emotional memories are triggered. Emotions that have to do with loss are triggered throughout our lives, often in the form of anniversary reactions.

Many people experience sadness when a relationship has ended. Within Chinese culture, researchers found the presence of love-related concepts such as "sad love." Love does not technically meet the criteria of an emotion, but can be described as an emotional state, a mood, or a mixture of emotions such as excitement, joy, happiness, or sensory pleasure. The disappointment of a relationship ending can lead you to experience anger as well as sadness. Maybe you should be angry when such things happen. Anger is the subject of the next chapter.

CHAPTER **11**

MAYBE YOU SHOULD BE ANGRY

Perhaps your phone was stolen, your best friend started dating the person you like, or you were put down by someone. In any case, you're angry and maybe that's exactly how you should feel.

Anger deserves appreciation. Designed to produce action in response to goals that are blocked, the violation of social norms, or to remedy situations that are wrong, anger alerts you to circumstances that are unjust and tells you that you're having a reaction to something that should not be as it is. In some situations, pain alone causes anger, regardless of the source of that pain (Izard, 1991). Often anger is thought to be a disruptive emotional force; however, it is a signal that alerts you to take action that is self-protective. So actually, anger is a good emotion that is sometimes misunderstood or misused. This is possibly due to the action tendency of anger, which includes a sense of physical strength, self-assurance, hostility, and strong impulsive feelings (Izard, 1991).

Getting caught up in how this emotion makes you feel and think may be part of the reason why people have difficulty regulating their anger responses and expressing them appropriately. When anger is triggered, your sympathetic nervous system creates arousal in the form of physical agitation, muscle tension, and strength that prepares your body for action. Blood pressure, body temperature, and heart rate increase—you feel hot. The impulse related to what you feel is to strike out at someone or something. Situations that elicit anger demand that you are physically ready to appear aggressive. Anger is designed to protect the self, and, in doing so, results in a greater willingness to take risks (Lerner & Keltner, 2001; Lerner & Tiedens, 2006). Given how anger makes you feel, your thoughts turn negative, which helps you to carry out the actions required— when you think negatively you can justify taking action.

RECOGNIZING ANGER TRIGGERS

It's important to pay attention to what exactly is triggering your anger and to protect yourself accordingly. In some situations expressing anger, rather than inhibiting it, might be counterproductive. Suppose someone you love or respect is emotionally hurtful to you. Your anger might jeopardize the relationship, especially if you want to lash out, get away, or make the other person experience guilt for how they made you feel. If you express your anger, the focus might then become your angry reaction and not how the other person's behavior activated it. In such a situation your anger is simply informing you to protect yourself from someone who is hurting you. But the importance of remaining attached to a person who is hurtful may get in the way of recognizing that the person to whom you are attached is, in fact, hurtful. Your anger may be trying to tell you so. In that case, the expression of hurt or sadness may be more productive in resolving the issue than expressing anger.

Shame is often a source of anger. Although the relationship between anger and shame is widely recognized, recent research has considered when anger is shame-related and when it is not (Hejdenberg & Andrews, 2011). Although it is often assumed that having an angry temperament is related to shame, this study refuted that effect for both men and women. According to the findings, shame is related to anger that is felt after specific provocation, such as criticism. Thus it is important to figure out what triggered your angry response, consider whether or not other emotions may be hiding behind your anger, and recognize that, ultimately, you have the ability to manage the action potential created by anger and decide how you will respond to situations.

A circumstance where intense anger was triggered—being humiliated, betrayed, or hurt in a relationship—may result in your anger being activated again whenever that circumstance is remembered. Your emotional system is simply doing its job by reminding you to protect yourself or find a solution. But you may not be able to let go of this anger until you understand why it is being activated, figure out what you can do differently now or in the future, or simply succeed in finding a reasonable ending in your favor.

ANGER AND EMPATHY

There is a complex relationship between anger and empathy—the ability to know what another person is feeling. Anger at someone seems to automatically inhibit your empathy for them, or, put another way, having empathy for another person interferes with expressing anger toward them. A perceived injustice requires action and necessitates that you are not inhibited about hurting someone else. Anger suppresses your empathy so that you can carry out the necessary interaction. What your anger is doing is rallying resources, both physical and cognitive, to stop someone who is doing whatever it is that may be threatening to you. Empathizing is akin to making excuses for behavior that has hurt you. Momentarily, anger will cut off your empathy for their pain and help you to focus on your own self-protection. Even so, how you express your anger—the ways in which you use its action tendency—is important, since exaggerated, inappropriate, or maladaptive anger expression will get in the way of the other person interpreting what you feel.

ANGER AND RETALIATION

Does getting back at someone who made you angry actually help you? The emotion of anger results in a willingness to endure the consequences of punishing someone who had betrayed you (de Quervain et al., 2004; O'Gorman, Wilson, & Miller, 2005). However, researchers have found that thinking about punishing someone, or even punishing them, will cause you to continue focusing on your anger towards that person (Carlsmith, Wilson, & Gilbert, 2008). So wanting revenge or seeking it can keep you from moving on and truly regaining the sense of yourself that was lost in the betrayal. It is highly likely that wanting revenge when you are wronged is a result of humiliation or shame that accompanies an injustice.

Anger can make you feel as though you want to lash out at someone or something because it automatically creates physiological responses and thoughts that prepare you to protect yourself. So if you follow through with your impulse to vent your anger, will you then be relieved? Many people think so, which perhaps is why, when their anger is triggered, they slug a pillow, punch a wall, kick anything in their way, vent their anger in an aggressive sports activity, or vicariously do so by watching a violent movie. Such expression of anger is known as *catharsis,* a term borrowed from Greek literature, which basically translates as emotional release or purification. However, a psychological researcher has found that venting to reduce anger is like using gasoline to put out a fire—it fuels aggressive thoughts, increases aggressive responding, and does not lead to a more positive mood (Bushman, 2002). In one experiment, people were best off doing nothing at all rather than venting their anger. The researcher concluded that distraction might be the best way to manage your anger until you calm down. So when you are angry you are better off if you pet your cat, watch a comedy program, or hang out with your friends.

Anger can also be *displaced*—a situation where you take out your anger on someone else. Imagine a situation where you became angry or annoyed at someone and then later are negative or hostile toward someone else. For example, you become angry with your coach and later snarl at a friend for no good reason. Psychologists refer to such behavior as *displaced aggression* because the target of your aggressive response is innocent. The possibility of displaced aggression may occur when you're angry if you are prone to *ruminate*— think about the situation over and over again. Researchers have found that the more you think about an annoying or anger-causing situation, the more you may end up in a negative mood that may affect your relationship with others (Bushman, Bonacci, Pedersen, Vasquez, & Miller, 2005). In fact, according to these researchers, the more you think about it, the greater the likelihood that you will take your anger or annoyance out on someone else. Take a deep breath, distract yourself, and don't hurt your relationships with others who care about you.

SUMMARY AND CONCLUSION

Anger is sometimes misunderstood or irrationally misused; however, it is meant to be an adaptive internal signal that cues self-protective action. When your goals are blocked, social norms are violated, situations are wrong, and when you are in pain, your response may be an angry one. Anger alerts you to circumstances that seem unjust or should not be as they are. Anger is designed to protect you, so when it is triggered you become physically agitated, tense, and strong. Your blood pressure, body temperature, and heart rate increase, your thoughts become negative, and you may have

Anger: What's It to You?

Do you think your anger needs to be better managed? Any emotion taken to an unhealthy level is dysfunctional, whether it's sadness, guilt, or even excitement. Anger management has to do with having sensible reactions to situations that elicit anger, and an ability to divert that anger into acceptable behaviors or deal with it in ways that are healthy. It's not that you shouldn't be angry, but anger does not have to result in expressed aggression.

You may not be able to do so at the moment you are angry, but it is useful to consider the source of your anger. You may find that your anger is in response to other emotions that have led you to experience vulnerability, such as sadness, shame, or guilt. Figuring out what is behind certain tendencies to express anger and what you can do differently may help you to respond more appropriately the next time it happens—and there will be a next time, since emotions are an essential part of being human.

Knowing that venting anger only stirs up your emotional brain, rather than calms it down, find ways to recover when anger consumes you. Rather than vent your anger, do something physical such as running or walking that will relieve the tension in your body. Even a warm shower could be a relief. Relieve your negative thoughts by distracting yourself with music or some enjoyable interaction with another person.

When anger is triggered you can strongly experience its action potential as your body tenses, you feel hot, and you become aware of negative thoughts. But along with the action potential of an emotion, you also have the capacity to quickly consider, inhibit, or amplify your response before you implement it. Being able to cognitively consider consequences, recognize a course of action that would resolve the situation, and respond in healthy, regulated ways are essential to using your emotions in the self-protective and informational purposes for which they are intended.

an impulse to strike out at someone or something. Your emotional system is simply doing its job by reminding you to protect yourself or find a solution. Thus, it is important to pay attention to what exactly is triggering your anger and to protect yourself accordingly. You are less likely to experience empathy toward a person when you are angry with them—not caring so much about how another person might feel makes it easier to express anger. Wanting revenge or seeking it is often a result of humiliation or shame that accompanies an injustice, however, it can keep you from moving on and truly regaining the sense of yourself that was lost in the betrayal.

Anger is a very strong negative emotion. Disgust is experienced similarly. Our next chapter is about the emotion of disgust. Prepare yourself to possibly experience that emotion as you read about what makes people disgusted.

CHAPTER *12*

DISGUST CAN MAKE YOU SICK

Melissa's friends teased her about her weird-fear, as they called it. Melissa's weird-fear affected her sitting in movie theater seats. When in a theater she would cover the seat with a garbage bag, which was fine with her friends as long as she didn't move around and make noise. If her friends decided to see a movie on the spur of the moment, Melissa would decline unless someone had a clean plastic bag that she could take with her. Since she could only sleep well in her own bed, which was another behavior related to her weird-fear, Melissa became upset if she had to stay at a hotel, and she simply refused to spend the night at a friend's home. You guessed correctly if you wondered if Melissa had ever been subjected to head lice. In fact, as a pre-teen she had contracted a head lice infestation, also known as *pediculosis capitis,* five times and she was definitely repulsed by the thought of it. Although the spread of head lice is uncommon, but possible, in the seats and beds avoided by Melissa, she was not taking any chances.

An emotion connected with our primitive brain, disgust is an emotion of avoidance. Disgust informs you to get away from something offensive, and can involve an intense rejection response of gagging or vomiting to ensure that you pay attention. The facial expression associated with a disgust response is unmistakable—your nose twists up, your mouth turns down, and your eyes squint (Ekman, 1982).

The avoidance response associated with disgust can, at times, appear instead as a phobia involving the emotions of fear or anxiety, as in Melissa's experience with head lice. A concern about being contaminated or infected by certain creatures such as rats, spiders, cockroaches, or maggots can evoke strong disgust reactions (Olatunji & Sawchuk, 2005). Similarly, people can experience disgust or anxiety, as well as have an avoidance response, to things they might consider to be unsanitary, such as public toilet seats, doorknobs, or an unclean restaurant.

You might understand why some people are afraid of spiders because of their appearance, the potential of some of them to bite, and the fact that they are just different from humans and likely misunderstood. Psychological science is still attempting to find what causes phobias (referred to as fears, but really anxieties) in people, such as those related to spiders. Researchers examined the degree to which the emotion of disgust motivates a person's avoidance of spiders and spider-related stimuli (Woody, McLean, & Klassen, 2005). They found that disgust sensitivity, as well as anxiety, is present in individuals with small animal phobias. Since disgust motivates avoidance, it makes sense that it is an important aspect of a spider phobia. The emotion of disgust may play a very important part in what makes people fearful of (or anxious about) spiders, especially since there was likely a time when such emotional responses served to protect humans.

DISGUST AND YOUR SENSES

Disgust is protective and your basic senses play a part in alerting your brain to trigger the emotion. You may be disgusted by what you smell, taste, touch, see, or hear. But you might also become disgusted by something that you are thinking! For example, you or someone you know might be considered a "picky eater," but this may be due to disgust sensitivity or a prior experience of disgust. Aversion to food that looks slimy, unfamiliar, or has a strange smell or texture is instinctual and self-protective since the emotion of disgust protects humans from eating anything that might be contaminated or spoiled. A previous experience in which you had a disgust response can later trigger another, even in your thoughts. When your brain assesses a situation based on a past experience, like becoming sick after eating a certain food, you can become repulsed by the thought of eating that food, such as when someone suggests it. Your brain is simply protecting you as emotional responses are supposed to do. This is why avoidance is the primary action you take when you are disgusted (Izard, 1993).

The emotion of disgust, as well as anxiety and happiness, can be activated by certain smells—referred to as *olfactory emotion elicitors*—whereas other basic emotions such as sadness, anger, fear, and surprise are not elicited through the sense of smell (Croy, Olgun, & Joraschky, 2011). Researchers wondered whether the smell of certain odors can affect how much we like particular people, places, and foods (Wrzesniewski, McCauley, & Rozin, 1999). They studied people's reactions to certain odors, and also to products that disguise body odor such as cologne and perfume. It turns out that your memory for certain odors does affect whether you like certain people, places, and foods. So if you love the smell of the chocolate chip cookies your grandmother makes, you might really like a place or food that smells similarly. But when it comes to scented products, your sense of smell may not decide if you like a person. According to that research study, you may like the smell of a cologne or perfume, but it doesn't cause you to evaluate the person who wears it more favorably. So, your emotional memory of a smell that's connected with something you enjoyed counts a lot. But spraying yourself with products won't necessarily make someone like you more.

MORAL DISGUST

Another version of a disgust response, known as moral disgust, has been shaped by legal, religious, and ethical concerns among humans. Certain human behaviors—such as child abuse, murder, rape, and racism—that violate a standard of conduct or do not uphold the social order can activate moral disgust (Olatunji & Sawchuk, 2005). Simply recognizing something that does not appear to be morally right can trigger a disgust response, such as discovering that a friend is cheating on a test, hearing about a person who tortures animals, or seeing your divorced mother or father kissing someone who is not your parent. The activation of moral disgust responses in people can contribute to their motivation to do what is considered to be right in their particular society, much like guilt or shame responses can maintain social order.

USING DISGUST AS ARMOR

Intentionally evoking disgust in another person can be a way to cope with, or disguise, one's own anxiety. In social situations some people will distract and push others away by behaving in a way that is disgusting to them—for example, with a loud burp, passing gas, or spitting. Such behavior can protect a person, though not appropriately, by evoking disgust in the observer. Given the consequences, as seen in the disgust responses of others, it might even be considered an aggressive or fearless attitude of disdain, condescension, or disregard for what other people think.

HUMOR AND DISGUST

The emotion of disgust can be a great source of amusement and connection when it is shared with others. If you encounter something disgusting when you are with a friend it can be amusing, whereas the same situation experienced alone will not be funny unless perhaps you describe it later to someone who appreciates the humor in your story. Things like finding a dead cockroach in your cereal are quite disgusting when you are alone, but can be pretty amusing when you are with someone who, hopefully along with you, is amused by their disgust response. In addition, many jokes are funny because they are designed to evoke a disgust response in the listener; these types of jokes are popularly known as "toilet humor."

Disgust: What's It to You?

Imagine you are in a situation where you experience disgust, but removing yourself from the situation would be inappropriate for the moment. Aside from acknowledging to yourself that disgust makes you want to get away, there are some things you can do to interfere with a disgust response.

Distracting yourself can help you recover quickly from a disgust response. If you focus on what has disgusted you then your body is more likely to respond in a rejecting way, including gagging or throwing up. Distract yourself with conversation or by thinking of something pleasant. Since disgust can be felt in your facial expression, changing your facial expression can interfere with your disgust response (Rozin & Fallon, 1987). For example, smiling can interfere with a disgust response and help you to recover from one. Altering your perspective on what is disgusting you can interfere with or change your response (Rozin & Fallon, 1987). When your reaction is to another person, use empathy. Rather than be disgusted by that person, instead try to feel sorry for him. Similarly, if something you smell or see is disgusting, try to take a scientific approach to it; for example, remind yourself that it is part of nature. In a situation of moral disgust, acknowledge that the situation just doesn't seem right, and that's why it triggered disgust. Talking about a situation that seems morally disgusting to you and attempting to understand your response can help.

SUMMARY AND CONCLUSION

Recognized across diverse cultures, disgust is triggered by something undesirable that you smell, taste, touch, see, or hear. Even a thought of something that disgusts you can activate a disgust response. Avoidance is the action people take when disgusted. It informs you to get away from something offensive, and can involve an intense rejection response of gagging or vomiting. Avoidance responses associated with disgust can instead appear as a phobia involving the emotions of fear or anxiety. Certain human behaviors that violate a standard of conduct or do not uphold the social order can activate moral disgust. Intentionally evoking disgust in another person can be a way to cope with, or disguise, one's own anxiety. Even so, disgust can be very amusing when you are with another person.

It's possible that you can attempt to hide other emotions that you feel toward another person by instead expressing that you are disgusted by them. Imagine being envious of another person, and, because you may think envy will make you look bad, you instead view the other person as morally disgusting in some way. Perhaps that would work. But maybe it would be better to find out more about the emotion of envy, what triggers it, and how to understand yourself when you feel envious. You will discover interesting facts about envy in the following chapter.

CHAPTER 13

THE SECRET LIFE OF ENVY

Brandon felt he was in love with Jasmine, but he kept it to himself since it was obvious that she really liked Travis. Playing it cool was essential so that Brandon wouldn't humiliate himself. Parties were especially torturous for him when both Jasmine and Travis were there. It was difficult not to envy Travis, who was intelligent, knew exactly what to say in social situations, and had a real sense of style in the way he dressed. Paying attention to Jasmine, who was always paying attention to Travis, was agonizing for Brandon. Rather than look around at anyone else, he was preoccupied with the thought that Travis and Jasmine would finally end up together. Brandon's silent envy of Travis was a painful addition to his disappointment about Jasmine's lack of interest in him and his feelings of inadequacy.

Envy is a secretly held emotion. If you are envious of another person it's unlikely that you will admit it to anyone, except perhaps to someone who might share your envy, help to raise you up, or be inclined to diminish the envied person. The emotion of envy can be triggered in circumstances that involve a social comparison where you perceive another person as having possessions, attributes, or attainments that diminish your own status (Silver & Sabini, 1978; Smith

& Kim, 2007). Comparisons with others are a part of the yardstick by which you measure yourself—your self-evaluation. Envy is triggered when you come up short in a comparison, which is part of the reason why it is experienced as such an unpleasant emotion. In order to adjust the measurements to neutralize your envy, you may devalue the other person, elevate yourself, or do both. However, in the case of Brandon, you may have wished that he would have just □□□□ □ □ □□□□ □□ his self-esteem and moved on.

Although it may seem that Brandon has become a bit obsessed with Jasmine and Travis, if you walk into a party and see someone you envy, it's likely that you will focus on information or details about that person and their behavior more than you will on others. The next day you might remember more about the person you envy than about anyone else at the party. Why would this be the case? Researchers found that people are more likely to think about a person they envy, pay attention to details about them, and correctly remember that information much more than they would with someone who is not envied (Hill, DelPriore, & Vaughan, 2011). Although it's bad enough that you might become preoccupied with someone you envy, there's more: the investigators also found that memories of the envied person interfered with participants' cognitive skills when they attempted to solve difficult word puzzles (Hill et al., 2011). So if you come across someone you envy, rather than focus on that person, use your willpower to focus on your own positive attributes and qualities. Focusing on the person you envy can negatively affect your thinking.

The emotion of envy is often confused with jealousy. Unlike envy, which has to do with wanting another person's qualities, success, or possession, jealousy has to do with thinking you will lose, or have lost, some affection or security from another person because of someone or something else. Jealousy is not considered an emotion; however, it can trigger intense emotions, such as envy, anxiety, or anger as self-protective responses that warn you of a threat to your relationship with a valued other person. More will be said about jealousy later in this chapter.

THE PURPOSE OF ENVY

Given that emotions have evolved to help us, what could possibly be the purpose of envy? First, consider the thoughts and feelings that envy creates: you want what someone else has, whatever it is that you envy in another person has limited availability, and the envied quality or possession gives the person who has it some advantage or power. Secondly, the thoughts and feelings that result when the emotion of envy is triggered can make you experience hostility toward another person and suffering within yourself. In prehistoric times, you might either defer to the envied other person, do something to eliminate him or her, or find a way to possess the desired quality for yourself. Although we are no longer cavemen, the same solutions, with some variation, seem to occur in the contemporary human mind. Thus, through social comparison, envy helps you come up with a solution, and hopefully you will choose a healthy one.

BEHAVIORS ASSOCIATED WITH ENVY

People idealize when they are envious. You can imagine that a quality or something possessed by someone else would bring you happiness or fulfillment. Thus, envy makes you feel as though you are lacking something that will lead you to be admired as much as you secretly admire the person who has the desired attribute or possession you envy. It's likely that one of the things you don't like about those you envy is that other people admire them.

Envy can make you preoccupied with comparison and repeatedly measure your self-worth against that of someone else. Although envy can motivate you to damage the position of the person who is envied, either in your imagination or in reality, envy can also make you work harder in order to attain what the envied person possesses. Some advertising agencies use envy as a marketing tool, since products sell best when they evoke envy in the consumer (van de Ven, Zeelenberg, & Pieters, 2009). Psychological researchers have found that attempts to gain envied social status can influence consumer choices, such as the desire for "green" products when shopping in public—but not in private—even when those products cost more than their non-green equivalents (Griskevicius, Tybur, & Van den Bergh, 2010).

Your envy does not always belong to you, but instead may originate from taking on what your parents envied or admired. For example, if your parents struggled financially and wished for more money, you might envy those who have it. Or if your parents wish they had a college education, you might admire those who do.

BEING ENVIED

But what if you are the person who is envied? We don't usually consider what it is like for those who are envied, but people who are the recipients of envy can feel uncomfortable. Imagine having someone dislike you, or even hate you, because you have an attribute, a possession, or a privilege that they want and are lacking. The things that trigger envy are the same things that could trigger admiration. Yet envy is tinged with hostility whereas the essence of admiration is warm, even if it also creates discomfort in those who are admired.

There are reasons to pay attention to whether or not another person envies you, particularly if you are involved in a negotiation, such as selling something you own to a peer. Researchers found that where social comparisons exist—for example, if your peer thinks your life is better than his own—envy is triggered, and that envy promotes deception in negotiation, and helps that other person justify their deceptive behavior (Moran & Schweitzer, 2008). Thus, envy can influence ethical decision making.

If someone envies you it can feel like a very uncomfortable compliment because of the hostility and resentment that accompany this emotion. However, there are ways to lessen the envy that someone might experience about you. Researchers have found that being helpful or friendly to a person who envies you is a strategy that can diminish the destructive effects of their envy (van de Ven, Zeelenberg, & Pieters, 2010). According to these researchers, people who fear being envied tend to behave in ways that are prosocial by helping others who might envy them. They speculate that people who are better off might use such an appeasement strategy to dampen the destructive effects of envy, and it can help to improve the situation of those who are not as well off.

ATTRACTION OR ENVY?

What might seem strange is that it is possible to mistake your envy of another person for attraction. The hostility that you might experience with envy of a competitor is missing in this instance because the expectation is that you will get the envied attribute by association. Thus, you can "fall in love" with what you want for yourself that another person has—status, power, or intelligence, for example—rather than with who that person really happens to be. You can imagine that you will get what you need by being attached to someone who has it. But if you idealize someone in this way you may later experience disappointment when you discover that they are not as great as you imagined them to be. By the time you come to your senses you may experience the hostile side of envy toward them that you hid from yourself.

ENVY AND YOUR SELF-DEFINITION

A big way in which you define yourself has to do with your ideals, ambitions, and what you value. Your ideal self is what you aspire to be, the best that you think you could or should be. Often this ideal comes from social comparisons. Your sense of self is constantly measuring itself against your ideals and coming to various conclusions. If you measure up, you feel good, excited, and even elated. If you don't measure up, you may feel disprooved or ashamed. Self esteem is determined to a great degree by your own comparison of your sense of self to your ideal self. However, it is sometimes easier to place that ideal onto someone else in the form of envy.

Your values and how you measure yourself against them are likely to change as you mature and as you learn to evaluate your potential and accept your limitations. If you have realistic ideals and can generally live up to them, your self-esteem will not be threatened. If your ideals are exaggerated and you cannot reach them, your good feelings from successes may be short-lived, you may feel that you are never good enough, and your envy of others may be constantly triggered.

SCHADENFREUDE

Determining how you feel about yourself can involve comparisons with others—evaluating yourself in relation to how fortunate or unfortunate you perceive others to be. When you envy another person and see them as having something or some quality you wish to have yourself, your status is lowered in your own mind. Figuring out who you are in relation to others can be complicated, and it may involve a painful feeling of inferiority when you are envious. Yet there is an aspect of envy that also involves pleasure. Gaining pleasure in another's misfortune is commonly referred to as *schadenfreude*—a German word that is similar to the concept of envy. However, where envy is focused more on the displeasure one might have in response to someone else's good fortune, schadenfreude pertains more to gaining pleasure from another's misfortune.

The relationship between envy and schadenfreude is seen, for example, in situations where envy of another person turns to pleasure when the envied person experiences a setback (Smith et al., 1996). If you consider that emotions serve to protect you, then the motivation to view oneself positively in social comparisons may lead people to experience pleasure in the misfortunes of others because it protects and enhances their own view of themselves (van Dijk, van Koningsbruggen, Ouwerkerk, & Wesseling, 2011).

JEALOUSY

Many people confuse the emotion of envy with jealousy, and much of the early research about these feeling states involved controversy about similarities or differences, and whether they are one emotion or two separate ones. However, significant differences between envy and jealousy are recognized; namely, jealousy involves a social triangle—generally three people, although you could be jealous of someone's interest in an activity that takes his or her time away from you—whereas envy is directed at one other person (Parrott, 1991). Jealousy is not considered by some researchers to be an emotion, but instead an emotional scene or plot that can trigger various emotions depending upon the circumstances (Ekman, 2003).

Various emotions can be triggered in response to the threat that jealousy creates. Some people become aggressive and offensive because of anger or anxiety that is triggered in response to threat. They want to hurt the person who is their jealous rival, and behave in ways that will control the person whose bond they might lose.

Other people retreat or withdraw from a relationship when they are jealous. Although their hope might be that the person with whom they have a relationship will notice and re-establish their bond, their retreat or withdrawal can trigger sadness or loneliness. Jealousy can also make you overwhelmed by uncertainty about the relationship and your insecurity can trigger anxiety that makes you worry or become obsessively preoccupied with the status of your relationship.

LEARNING ABOUT YOURSELF FROM JEALOUSY

When you experience jealousy, you have an opportunity to learn about yourself by asking yourself some questions: Are you perceiving that you are lacking in some quality that you would like to develop for yourself? Are you experiencing jealousy because, actually, you want something more from your relationship that you are unable to obtain from that person, whether it is attention, fun, or being more exclusive? What do you think of yourself and who do you want to be? Being close to others can trigger the emotion of jealousy, especially if you do not value yourself or have experienced childhood loss or abandonment. However, recognize that your feelings have more to do with your relationship with yourself than with your relationship with someone else.

SUMMARY AND CONCLUSION

Social comparisons can trigger envy. Envy can lead you to become preoccupied with making comparisons and repeatedly measuring your self-worth against that of someone else. The envied quality of someone else appears to give the person who has it some advantage or power, and can make you experience hostility toward that person and suffering within yourself. If you envy another person, you likely imagine that a quality or possession of that person would bring you happiness or

Envy: What's It to You?

Envy has to do with feeling unhappy about someone else's success, possession, or qualities, and, at the same time, secretly feeling inferior yourself.
Instead of finding success for yourself or improving yourself, you may be
envious and want what another person has, or find yourself wishing that
the other person would lose that quality or possession in order to make
things seem fair. If you are envious of someone, you may want to put him
down, as though this will raise you up or lower everyone else's opinion of
him. But it just doesn't work! We really can't know what another person's
life is like, but an envious person assumes that the other person is happier
or better. So, in a strange way, when you envy someone else, you are giving that person a compliment. But it's a compliment that can harm you and
how you feel about yourself.

   When you experience envy, let it inform you to find ways to lift yourself
up rather than occupy yourself with a negative reaction to someone else.
Discover ways in which you can activate the emotions of pride or interest in
yourself, which are great antidotes to envy. Consider how you are regarding
the life of the person you envy. Likely your perception is based on your own
fantasy of who they are rather than the reality of their life.

fulfillment. It is no wonder that some advertising agencies use envy as a
marketing tool! Triggers that have to do with envy are similar to those
of admiration, but admiration lacks the hostility of envy. There are significant differences between envy and jealousy. Unlike envy, jealousy
involves a social triangle and can lead you to become overwhelmed by
uncertainty about the relationship and its status.

   Rather than envy another person, it would certainly be a relief
if you could just be interested in them instead. Interest is a highly
motivating emotion and it can help you to pursue your goals in
many ways. What causes you to be interested? You'll find out in
the next chapter how the emotion of interest can be useful to you.

CHAPTER 14

INTEREST IS MORE EXCITING THAN YOU THINK

Angelica admired her mother's friend, Katie, who was a lawyer. She thought about becoming a lawyer, even though she didn't know exactly what Katie did at work. Even so, Angelica admired Katie's intelligence, poise, and sense of humor. One summer Angelica had an opportunity to work in Katie's law office. After eight weeks observing the firm's lawyers reading over contracts and writing reports, Angelica didn't think it interested her in the least. She was stuck with figuring out a new path for herself. On the last day of her summer work, Katie took Angelica out to lunch. Angelica decided to honestly, but kindly, convey her lack of interest in what went on in the office. As a result, Angelica and the attorney began to brainstorm about what Angelica loved to do—writing, doing creative activities, influencing decisions, and being involved in high energy situations. Fortunately, Angelica's mentor was able to direct her toward many possible careers that fit what she loved to do, including other areas of legal work.

If asked to think of specific emotions, interest may not top your list. Yet in terms of the motivational aspect of emotion, interest is critically important: you are more likely to finish an interesting novel than a boring one, to want to be with a person who garners your attention as opposed to someone who doesn't, and to be more engaged in learning and recreational activities that hold your interest than those that do not. Like Angelica, you may think about what you want to be, such as a chemist, a physician, or a journalist. But in terms of the emotion of interest, perhaps it is even more important to think about what you love to do.

Interest is activated when your brain appraises a situation or event with simultaneous desire, or a perceived need to expend effort (Keltner & Lerner, 2010). Therefore, figuring out what you enjoy doing is an important part of determining your goals.

More than 100 years ago, an educator named Felix Arnold (1906) wrote about the psychology of interest and its importance to teaching. Interest, he pointed out, is related to desire, excitement, feeling, attention, and goal seeking. Yet controversy existed in Arnold's era, as it does now, as to whether or not educators should concern themselves with making subject matter more interesting for the sake of engaging their students in the learning process.

Many years later, researchers found that interest is related to, and motivates, excitement, exploration, attention, perception, and challenge (Deci & Ryan, 1985; Izard, 1977). When you are interested you are fascinated, curious, and engaged (Izard, 1977). A positive feeling that is associated with an activity is usually thought of as enjoyment, although the emotions of interest and enjoyment are thought to be different. Enjoyment of an activity, for example, is considered to have more of a rewarding function, while interest functions as a motivation to become involved in that activity (Tompkins, 1962).

EARLY INTEREST TRIGGERS

Very young infants have been found to direct their gaze to the human face, and this interest expression is associated with a decelerated heart rate that indicates a calming effect (Langsdorf, Izard, Rayias,

& Hembree, 1983). It's no wonder that people seem so inclined to smile and make faces at babies while talking to them—it is a natural way to engage an infant's interest and it can be calming when they are upset. A decrease in an infant's heart rate when interest is activated, aside from being associated with a quieting response, also promotes cognitive development, and creates an optimal condition for receiving information through the senses (Izard, 1977; Silvia, 2001). If we are hard-wired to be interested or curious, this would serve to develop our intellect and knowledge of the world.

INTEREST AND PERFORMANCE

Situations that attract the senses, such as change, movement, and novelty can activate interest, focus your attention, and maintain your attention while you make an effort to explore, understand, and learn (Izard, 1977). However, there are many tasks or activities that you may not feel very motivated to do. How do you muster up the motivation to do something that seems boring?

Speculating that individuals regulate their interest levels and motivation to perform necessary activities, researchers wondered if people had specific strategies they used in order to enhance their performance on boring tasks (Sansone, Weir, Harpster, & Morgan, 1992). The results of three studies found that by intentionally engaging in certain behaviors that increased the interest value of the activity, individuals improved the likelihood of performing an uninteresting activity. The researchers concluded that people who use strategies to make an activity more interesting will view the activity more positively. However, one of the implications of the studies was that individuals may attempt to make an activity more interesting even if it results in some cost to performance. For example, you might try to make a class more interesting by making a clever joke about something that is being taught, even though it may potentially result in a reprimand by the instructor. So, when someone is acting out in class it is possible that they are just trying to create interest. If you are the one who is asking someone to perform a boring activity, like cleaning up after a party, it is important to build in some ways in which they can increase their interest—perhaps listening to loud music or maybe even including some breaks for off-task but interesting behavior, such as a pillow fight.

In learning situations, interest can help you or it can possibly get in your way. A study of the effect of interest on attention and learning took a look at individuals studying reading material (Shirey & Reynolds, 1988). Although sentences in the readings that were most interesting were learned better, less attention was paid to them as a strategy for learning the material. The individuals who were effective at learning the material read the more interesting sentences faster than the less interesting ones. They gave more attention to information that required extra effort, and were better able to identify important information in the text. For example, the more effective readers were able to sort out sentences that were written in a more interesting way but had less important information from those that had information they considered important to remember. So if you are reading material for a test, you may be inclined to focus on those sentences that are appealing to you and dismiss those that are not. However, according to these researchers, you may benefit by doing the opposite since you will most likely remember the interesting material, but the boring stuff is what needs your attention for effective performance.

INTEREST AND INTERESTS

When the emotion of interest is triggered it can potentially serve as a foundation to developing interests (Silvia, 2001). Suppose, for example, that you happen to observe a person doing something that

Interest: What's It to You?

It's possible to be interested in, or curious about, so many things that making a choice becomes confusing, frustrating, and leads you to feel that there are too many choices and you can't seem to center on just one of them. Having to follow one interest among many may be somewhat like going to a great restaurant and wanting to try all of the main courses, even though you must choose among them. Thus, you will end up choosing one and hopefully will have an opportunity to compare it to others at another time. As you might expect, when the novelty wears off of something that triggered your interest it may not provide enjoyment that keeps you involved. Thus, you may want to move on or find a way to make the situation more interesting.

Highly stimulating activities that continuously trigger interest—for some people, these may include video games or social events—can erroneously lead you to think that everyday situations that could be interesting are instead boring by comparison. This may also be applied to relationships. For example, if you are in a relationship that has a lot of high drama it might hold your interest more than a peaceful and healthy one. So it is important to assess a situation or a relationship in terms of whether or not it is healthy for you or simply holding your interest because it is unpredictable. On the other hand, in both activities and relationships, you may want to find ways to trigger your interest when a situation does not provide excitement. In terms of a relationship, having common interests may be a way to remain interesting to one another.

Expanding your knowledge of the world, people, or any subject can make you a more interesting person and also activate your interest in a variety of new things. In addition, being interested in other people—how they think and feel, what they like to do, or what they know—and sharing information with them will make them more interesting to you and will lead them to find you more interesting.

---

seems exciting to you. Your interest is aroused. You might then be motivated to learn more about the subject, engage in activities that pertain to it, or even focus your future studies in that direction. The emotion of interest has a thought-action tendency that causes you to think about what has stimulated your interest and creates an inclination to investigate or expand your knowledge (Izard, 1977). Considering the potential long-term impact of interest, it would seem that having new experiences, or being curious about possibilities that exist in the world, can lead you to find a focus in life that is enjoyable to you

SUMMARY AND CONCLUSION

Interest is activated when your brain appraises a situation or event with pleasantness, desire, or a perceived need to expend effort. Interest motivates excitement, exploration, attention, perception, and challenge. The emotions of interest and enjoyment are thought to be different even though they are related in various ways. The emotion of interest serves to develop our intellect and knowledge of the world. Situations that attract the senses, such as change, movement, and novelty, can activate interest, as well as focus and maintain attention. When interest is triggered it can potentially serve as a foundation to developing interests. Highly stimulating activities that continuously trigger interest can erroneously lead you to think that everyday situations that could be interesting are instead boring by comparison. In both activities and relationships, you may want to find ways to trigger your interest when a situation does not provide excitement. Having common interests in a relationship may be a way to remain interesting to one another.

Perhaps you are trying to find happiness through your interests. Happiness is an interesting emotion and I hope you enjoy reading about it in the following chapter.

CHAPTER **15**

HAPPINESS CAN MAKE YOU SMILE OR CRY

Austin had worked hard to write the essay he would enter into the literary competition. Then he tore it up. He had written about himself in an intellectual way, and the story didn't really describe who he was or what he felt. Starting fresh, he decided that he would rather write the painful truth about his experiences as a foster child, his later adoption, and what he felt—completely numb—when he saw his drug-addicted biological mother last year. It seemed risky, but it also felt right to be his authentic self. When Austin received notice that he won the first place award, he was elated, but something felt unreal, as though he couldn't quite hold onto the recognition that he had won. At the same time, he wanted to tell everyone, as though saying it would validate the reality for him. He won! And he couldn't believe it. Austin put his head in his hands and he began sobbing.

Why would Austin cry at such a happy ending? We expect that people might cry when they are sad, physically or emotionally hurt, sympathizing or empathizing with another person who is suffering, or in response to a joyful event. One theory about why people cry at happy endings involves the notion that people unconsciously hold back their emotions until it is relatively safe to express them

(Weiss & Sampson, 1986). For example, suppose you are watching a very sad movie and don't shed a tear during the parts that are sad, but cry at the happy ending. According to this theory, at a happy ending, when you are no longer threatened by the sadness and can safely experience it, the energy that is used to hold back the emotion of sadness is then lifted and the expression is relieving. Although, as the theorists note, this is likely only one of many reasons why people cry at happy endings, such paradoxical behavior is fascinating. It's possible in Austin's situation that sadness for himself, and even for his biological mother, wasn't really safe for him to experience emotionally until the later happy moment.

EMOTIONS OF HAPPINESS

There are many emotions that have to do with happiness, including elation, gladness, relief, joy, bliss, and amusement. Although these happy emotions all differ in terms of how they are experienced, they are represented by a similar facial expression: a smile (Ekman, 2003). Happy emotions provide an immediate but brief surge of pleasure of varying degrees and quality, and, like all other emotions, they motivate you.

Positive emotional states, such as happiness, that are both a personality characteristic and a result of past successes, have been found to lead to behaviors that in turn often lead to further success (Lyubomirsky, King, & Diener, 2005). However, this may not be true in all cultures.

Primarily in Western culture, emotions that are uplifting, such as joy, elation, amusement, or gladness, are considered to be positive and are associated with individual success, good health, and high self-esteem. Although Westerners may assume that all people should strive to experience more positive emotion in their lives, this may not be the case for other cultures, according to researchers

Janxin Leu, Jennifer Wang, and Kelly Koo (2011). These researchers point out that in many Asian cultural contexts, for example, happiness may be associated with negative social consequences, such as jealousy in others. In cultures informed by the Buddhist belief that pure pleasantness is impossible to attain or can lead to suffering, the goal may be moderation of positive emotion, instead of maximization. The researchers found that culture makes a difference in the role that positive emotions play in mental health, and that positive emotions may not be as positive for Asians as for European Americans. Emotion moderation through balancing positive and negative emotions may be a cultural goal in Asian contexts, whereas in Western contexts maximizing positive emotions may be a cultural goal. Thus it is always important to consider cultural differences, including the beliefs people have about positive emotions.

EMOTIONS THAT CREATE HAPPINESS

Understandably, the focus of emotion researchers has not been on the details of happy emotions as much as on those that create upset in people. In many instances, distinctly happy emotions fall under the general designation as positive emotions or are considered as happiness. Some of the attempts to distinguish these happy emotions from one another, as we do with the less pleasant emotions, such as anger, sadness, and disgust, may be useful to our understanding of the variety of situations and events that trigger them.

Elation. An event that fulfills a personal fantasy about the possibility of something amazing happening to you will trigger elation—the experience of unreality, euphoria, and confidence that makes you want to jump, shout, and announce the good news (DeRivera, Possell, Verette, & Weiner, 1989). You might experience elation upon finding out that something you had deeply wished for has come true.

Gladness and Relief. In contrast to elation, the emotion of gladness is created by a long nurtured hope that is fulfilled, and it is experienced as relaxation and relief (DeRivera et al., 1989). But relief itself is considered to be a happy or positive emotion. Relief is felt when something that had strongly stirred up your emotions subsides (Ekman, 2003). You may be familiar with the common expression of relief, a sigh, which seems to suggest that whatever has impacted you is let out in one deep breath.

Joy. The emotion of joy involves situations where there is a meaningful encounter—your heart feels "open" and you have a greater caring about others that seems to affirm life's meaning (DeRivera et al., 1989). Joy might be felt in a situation with others that you perceive to be a unique and pleasurable shared experience, and it is often accompanied by feelings of vigor, strength, and a readiness to engage in interpersonal interactions (DeRivera et al., 1989; Frija, 1986; Izard, 1977). You are likely to experience joy when, at a family event, you see a relative you love very much whom you have not seen in a long time. It is possible that religious or spiritual connections, ones that do not involve other living people, can trigger joy as well.

Bliss. A surge of extreme pleasure is felt when the emotion of bliss is activated. This state of rapture where you transcend yourself—

the feeling described by the expression "being on cloud nine"—is thought to be an intense experience. Love, sensory or sexual pleasure, anticipation of great excitement, or a meditative state are often felt as bliss (Ekman, 2003). Romantic love is often experienced as blissful when you are physically close to the person who is the object of your affection. When a blissful state is experienced with someone you love, the craving and need to recreate it can be intense.

Amusement. Amusement is the emotion felt in response to something funny or in reaction to other matters that have a humorous quality (Ekman, 2003). Amusement is usually associated with laughter. What makes something funny can vary among people and cultures, so it is impressive that screenwriters or authors can create material that is humorous to a large audience. Many situations or events that are amusing when you are with a friend or a group of friends are not at all amusing when you are alone, such as stepping on bubble gum on the sidewalk or seeing a huge rat jump out of a garbage bin. Tripping and falling into a mud puddle while wearing your good clothes may not be amusing at the time, but it could be amusing when you describe it, in retrospect, to another person.

WORKING ON HAPPINESS

You may want to be happier but think that anything you do won't make a difference. Researchers wondered themselves if the intentional pursuit of greater happiness could succeed if it was done under optimal conditions (Lyubomirsky, Dickerhoof, Boehm, & Sheldon, 2011). In their experiment they used two activities that are thought to be effective in enhancing happiness. One of the activities had to do with practicing optimistic thinking by visualizing your best possible future self, and the other had to do with expressing gratitude through writing. Participants in the study were people who intended to use the intervention to become happier, and were motivated to put effort into the activities involved in the intervention. The results of the study indicated that positive experiences and continued effort certainly do make a difference in boosting well-being when participants are informed about the happiness intervention, endorse it, and are committed to it. Even happiness requires effort.

It's understandable why people would want to be happier, and you might expect that if you value happiness, you might be more likely to pursue and attain it. But researchers have found that valuing happiness might be self-defeating, since the more you value happiness the more likely you might be to experience disappointment when you're not happy (Mauss, Tamir, Anderson, & Savino, 2011). Although we often hear the recommendation that one should have goals in mind and attempt to achieve them, this may not be true when it comes to happiness. For instance, if you want to participate in a triathlon, you know exactly what you must do and how hard you must practice and push yourself in order to achieve your goal. But happiness is not so tangible, and the goals that define happiness differ among people. Even so, it would be great to know exactly what to do, how to do it, and how often to do something in order to be happier. The researchers in this study found that people who highly value happiness may set standards for it that are hard to achieve, and when people cannot obtain the standards that they have set for themselves they are bound to be disappointed (Mauss et al., 2011). The researchers conclude that in the case of wanting happiness, people may feel worse off the more they want it, and that valuing or overvaluing happiness can possibly lead you to be less happy, even if happiness is within your reach. Perhaps this is a way in which happiness, or wanting happiness, can make you sad.

Happiness: What's It to You?

Have you ever noticed that people who often have a smile on their face seem to be happy? Do you think smiling can make you happier? While happiness creates a smiling facial expression, it is also true that a facial expression that closely resembles the pattern of muscles that are used to express happiness can cause you to experience a corresponding emotion (Ekman, 1993). Some theorists maintain that you do not even have to cognitively know that you have a particular expression on your face for the "facial feedback effect" to occur; that is, the physiology of a particular facial expression can affect your emotional experience (Ekman, Levenson, & Friesen, 1983; Strack, Stepper, & Martin, 1988). You might want to try it by loosely holding a clean pen or straw with your teeth, parallel to your mouth. The facial expression created is similar to a smile—an expression of happiness—and the facial feedback effect can trigger a positive emotional response in your brain. Assuming you want to be happy, it certainly can't hurt to put a smile on your face (at appropriate times, of course).

SUMMARY AND CONCLUSION

Emotions that have to do with happiness include elation, gladness, relief, joy, bliss, and amusement. Happy emotions differ in terms of how they are experienced, although they share a similar smiling facial expression. Positive, happy emotions are motivating and provide pleasure. Although less emphasis has been placed on distinguishing positive emotions from one another, they do vary in terms of intensity and the events that trigger them. Where elation has to do with an event that fulfils a personal fantasy, gladness is created by a less intense hope that is fulfilled and is related to the emotion of relief. You might imagine that your heart is more open when you experience joy in a situation that you perceive to be pleasurable and unique. In contrast, a surge of extreme pleasure is felt when the emotion of bliss is activated. In response to a humorous situation or to something that you perceive is funny, you will be amused. Given that you smile when you are happy, recreating the pattern of muscles that are used to express happiness can cause you to feel it.

CONCLUSION

Emotions are a powerful and extraordinary part of being human. Rather than focus on emotions only when they are disordered, I've attempted throughout this book to help you recognize how emotions can provide you with information, direct your attention, motivate your behavior, protect you, and help you to reach your goals. Now when an emotion is activated, you can make better sense of your feelings just by asking yourself a few questions, such as: Why did my appraisal system trigger that specific emotion, and what is the action potential of the emotion directing me to do? Is it correct for the situation or exaggerated? Did my brain possibly consider a past situation when it decided to trigger the emotion in the present circumstance? Is the emotion letting me know something I'd prefer to ignore? And I hope, along with me, you will continue to learn about emotions and what they can tell you. What's it to you? Everything!

REFERENCES

American Psychiatric Association. (2000). *Diagnostic and statistical manual of mental disorders* (Revised, 4th ed.). Washington, DC: Author.

Anderson, C., Horowitz, L., & French, R. (1983). Attributional style of lonely and depressed people. *Journal of Personality and Social Psychology, 45*(1), 127–136.

Archer, J. (2001). Broad and narrow perspectives in grief theory: Comment on Bonanno and Kaltman (1999). *Psychological Bulletin, 127*(4), 554–560.

Arnold, F. (1906). The psychology of interest (I). *The Psychological Review, 13*(4), 221–238.

Atkinson, J. (1957). Motivational determinants of risk-taking behavior. *Psychological Review, 64*, 359–372.

Averill, J. R. (1994). The eyes of the beholder. In P. Ekman & R. J. Davidson (Eds.), *The nature of emotion* (pp. 7–14). New York, NY: Oxford University Press.

Baumeister, R. F., & Leary, M. R. (1995). The need to belong: Desire for interpersonal attachments as a fundamental human motivation. *Psychological Bulletin, 117*(3), 497–529.

Baumeister, R. F, Stillwell, A. M., & Heatherton, T. F. (1994). Guilt: An interpersonal approach. *Psychological Bulletin, 115*(2), 243–267

Benedetti, F., Mayberg, H., Wager, T., Stohler, C., & Zubieta, J. (2005). Neurobiological mechanisms of the placebo effect. *Journal of Neuroscience, 25*(45), 10390–10402.

Birney, R., Burdick, H., & Teevan, R. (1969). *Fear of failure*. New York, NY: Van Nostrand Reinhold.

Bonanno, G. A., & Kaltman, S. (1999). Toward an integrative perspective on bereavement. *Psychological Bulletin, 125*(6), 760–776.

Bowlby, J. (1963). Pathological mourning and childhood morning. *Journal of the American Psychoanalytic Association, 11*(3), 500–541.

Bracha, H., Ralston, T. C., Matsukawa, J. M., Matsunaga, S., Williams, A. F., & Bracha, A. S. (2001). Does "fight or flight" need updating? *Psychosomatics, 45*, 118–449

Brown, B. H., Richards, H. C., & Wilson, C. A. (1996). Pet bonding and pet bereavement among adolescents. *Journal of Counseling & Development, 74*, 505–510.

Bruininks, P., & Malle, B. (2005). Distinguishing hope from optimism and related affective states. *Motivation and Emotion, 29*(4), 325–355.

Bushman, B. (2002). Does venting anger feed or extinguish the flame? Catharsis, rumination, distraction, anger, and aggressive responding. *Personality and Social Psychology Bulletin, 28*(6), 724–731.

Bushman, B., Bonacci, A., Pedersen, W., Vasquez, E., & Miller, N. (2005). Chewing on it can chew you up: Effects of rumination on triggered displaced aggression. *Journal of Personality and Social Psychology, 88*(6), 969–983.

Cannon, W. (1929). *Bodily changes in pain, hunger, fear, and rage.* New York, NY: Appleton-Century-Crofts.

Carlsmith, K. M., Wilson, T. D., & Gilbert, D. T. (2008). The paradoxical consequences of revenge. *Journal of Personality and Social Psychology, 95*, 1316–1324.

Cattell, R., & Scheier, I. (1961). *The meaning and measurement of neuroticism and anxiety.* New York, NY: Ronald.

Cavanaugh, L., Cutright, K., Luce, M., & Bettman, J. (2011). Hope, pride, and processing during optimal and nonoptimal times of day. *Emotion, 11*(1), 38–46.

Chepenik, L., Cornew, L., & Farah, M. (2007). The influence of sad mood on cognition. *Emotion, 7*(4), 802–811.

Chu, A. H. C., & Choi, J. N. (2005). Rethinking procrastination: Positive effects of "active" procrastination behavior on attitudes and performance. *Journal of Social Psychology, 14*, 245–264.

Clore, G. (1994). Why emotions are felt. In P. Ekman & R. J. Davidson (Eds.), *The nature of emotion: Fundamental questions* (pp.103–111). New York, NY: Oxford University Press.

Clore, G., & Ortony, A. (2008). Appraisal theories: How cognition shapes affect into emotion. In M. Lewis & J. M. Haviland-Jones (Eds.), *Handbook of emotions* (3rd ed., pp. 742–756). New York, NY: Guilford Press

Croy, I., Olgun, S., & Joraschky, P. (2011). Basic emotions elicited by odors and pictures. *Emotion, 11*(6), 1331–1335.

Darby, R., & Harris, C. (2010). Embarrassment's effect on facial processing. *Cognition and Emotion, 24*(7), 1157–1250.

Davis, M., & Franzoi, S. (1986). Adolescent loneliness, self-disclosure, and private self-consciousness: A longitudinal investigation. *Journal of Personality and Social Psychology, 51*, 595–608.

Deci, E., & Ryan, R. (1985). *Intrinsic motivation and self-determination in human behavior.* New York, NY: Plenum Press.

DeMartini, K., & Carey, K. (2011). The role of anxiety sensitivity and drinking motives in predicting alcohol use: A critical review. *Clinical Psychology Review, 31*(1), 169–177.

deQuervain, D., Fischbacher, U., Treyer, V., Schellhammer, M., Schnyder, U., Buck, A., & Fehr, E. (2004). The neural basis of altruistic punishment. *Science, 305*(5688), 1254–58.

DeRivera, J., Possell, L., Verette, J., & Weiner, B. (1989). Distinguishing elation, gladness, and joy. *Journal of Personality and Social Psychology, 57*(6), 1015–1023.

DeWall, C., Maner, J., & Rouby, D. (2009). Social exclusion and early-stage interpersonal perception: Selective attention to signs of acceptance. *Journal of Personality and Social Psychology, 96*(4), 729–741.

Dijk, C., Koenig, B., Ketelaar, T., & de Jong, P. (2011). Saved by the blush: Being trusted despite defecting. *Emotion, 11*(2), 313–319.

Drummond, P., & Lance, J. (1997). Facial flushing and sweating mediated by the sympathetic nervous system. *Brain, 110*, 793–803.

Ekman, P. (1982). *Emotion in the human face* (2nd ed.). New York, NY: Cambridge University Press.

Ekman, P. (1992). Are there basic emotions? *Psychological Review, 99*(3), 550–553.

Ekman, P. (1993). Facial expression and emotion. *American Psychologist, 48*, 384–392.

Ekman, P. (1994). Moods, emotions, and traits. In P. Ekman & R. Davidson (Eds.), *The nature of emotion: Fundamental questions* (pp. 15–19). New York, NY: Oxford University Press.

Ekman, P. (1999). Basic emotions. In T. Dalgleish & M. Power (Eds.), *Handbook of cognition and emotion* (pp. 45–60). New York, NY: Wiley.

Ekman, P. (2003). *Emotions revealed: Recognizing faces and feelings to improve communication and emotional life.* New York, NY: Holt.

Ekman, P., Levenson, R., & Friesen, W. (1983). Autonomic nervous system activity distinguishes among emotions. *Science, 221,* 1208–1210.

Elliot, A., & Thrash, T. (2004). The intergenerational transmission of fear of failure. *Personality and Social Psychology Bulletin, 30*(8), 957–971.

Epstein, S. (1994). Integration of the cognitive and the psychodynamic unconscious. *American Psychologist, 49,* 709–724.

Fernandez Slezak, D., & Sigman, M. (2011). Do not fear your opponent: Suboptimal changes of a prevention strategy when facing stronger opponents. *Journal of Experimental Psychology: General,* 1–12.

Fortune, J. L., & Newby-Clark, I. R. (2008). My friend is embarrassing me: Exploring the guilty by association effect. *Journal of Personality and Social Psychology, 95,*1440–1449.

Fredrickson, B. L., & Branigan, C. (2001). Positive emotions. In T. J. Mayne & G. A. Bonanno (Eds.), *Emotions: Current issues and future directions* (pp. 123–151). New York, NY: Guilford Press.

Fredrickson, B. L., & Cohn, M. (2008) Positive emotions. In M. Lewis & J. M. Haviland-Jones (Eds.), *Handbook of emotions* (3rd ed., pp. 777–796). New York, NY: Guilford Press.

Freud, S. (1961a). Civilization and its discontents. In J. Strachey (Ed. & Trans.), *The standard edition of the complete psychological works of Sigmund Freud* (Vol. 21, pp. 64–148). London, England: Vintage. (Original work published 1930)

Freud, S. (1961b). Mourning and melancholia. In J. Strachey (Ed. & Trans.), *The standard edition of the complete psychological works of Sigmund Freud* (Vol. 14, pp. 237–258). London, England: Vintage. (Original work published 1917)

Frija, N. (1986). *The emotions.* Cambridge, England: Cambridge University Press.

Gilovich, T., Medvec, V., & Savitsky, K. (2000). The spotlight effect in social judgment: An egocentric bias in estimates of the salience of one's own actions and appearance. *Journal of Personality and Social Psychology, 78*(2), 211–222.

Griskevicius, V., Tybur, J., & Van den Bergh, B. (2010). Going green to be seen: Status, reputation, and conspicuous conservation. *Journal of Personality and Social Psychology, 98,* 392–404.

Hejdenberg, J., & Andrews, B. (2011). The relationship between shame and different types of anger: A theory-based investigation. *Personality and Individual Differences, 50*(8), 1278–1282.

Henretty, J., Levitt, H., & Mathews, S. (2008). Clients' experiences of moments of sadness in psychotherapy: A grounded theory analysis. *Psychotherapy Research, 18*(3), 243–255.

Hill, S., DelPriore, D., & Vaughan, P. (2011). The cognitive consequences of envy: Attention, memory, and self-regulatory depletion. *Journal of Personality and Social Psychology, 101*(4) 653–666.

Hoffman, M. (1982). Development of prosocial motivation: Empathy and guilt. In N. Eisenberg (Ed.), *The development of prosocial behavior* (pp. 281–313). San Diego, CA: Academic Press.

Horowitz, L., French, R., & Anderson, C. (1982). The prototype of a lonely person. In L. Peplau & D. Perlman (Eds.), *Loneliness: A sourcebook of current theory, research, and therapy* (pp. 183–204). New York, NY: Wiley.

Izard, C. (1977). *Human emotions.* New York, NY: Plenum Press.

Izard, C. (1991). *The psychology of emotions.* New York, NY: Plenum Press.

Izard, C. (1993). Organizational and motivational functions of discrete emotions. In M. Lewis & J. M. Haviland (Eds.), *Handbook of emotions.* New York, NY: Guilford Press.

Johnson, D., & Fowler, J. (2011). The evolution of overconfidence. *Nature, 477,* 317–320.

Jones, W. H., Freemon, J., & Goswick, R. (1981). The persistence of loneliness: Self and other determinants. *Journal of Personality, 49*(1), 27–48.

Jones, W. H., & Kugler, K. (1993). Interpersonal correlates of the guilt inventory. *Journal of Personality Assessment, 61*(2), 246–258.

Keltner, D., & Anderson, C. (2000). Saving face for Darwin: The functions and uses of embarrassment. *Current directions in psychological science, 9*(6), 187–192.

Keltner, D., & Buswell, B. (1996). Evidence for the distinctness of embarrassment, shame, and guilt: A study of recalled antecedents and facial expressions of emotion. *Cognition and Emotion, 10,* 155–171.

Keltner, D., & Buswell, B. (1997). Embarrassment: Its distinct form and appeasement functions. *Psychological Bulletin, 122*(3), 250–270.

Keltner, D., & Lerner, J. (2010). Emotion. In D. Gilbert, S. Fiske, & G. Lindsey (Eds.), *Handbook of social psychology* (5th ed., pp. 317–352). New York, NY: McGraw Hill.

Kubler-Ross, E. (1969). *On death and dying* New York, NY. Routledge.

Lang, P., Davis, M., & Ohman, A. (2000). Fear and anxiety: animal models and human cognitive psychophysiology. *Journal of Affective Disorders, 61*, 137–159.

Langsdorf, P., Izard, C., Rayias, M., & Hembree, E. (1983). Interest expression, visual fixation, and heart rate changes in 2- to 8-month old infants. *Developmental Psychology, 19*(3), 375–386.

Lazarus, R. (1984). On the primacy of cognition. *American Psychologist, 39*(2), 124–129.

Lazarus, R. (1991). *Emotion and adaptation.* New York, NY: Oxford University Press.

Lazarus, R. (1994). Universal antecedents of the emotions. In P. Ekman & R. J. Davidson (Eds.), *The nature of emotion: Fundamental questions* (pp. 163–171). New York, NY: Oxford University Press.

Lazarus, R. (1999). Hope: An emotion and a vital coping resource against despair. *Social Research, 66*(2), 653–678.

Leary, M., & Kowalski, R. (1995). *Social anxiety.* London, England: Guildford Press.

LeDoux, J. (1996). *The emotional brain.* New York, NY: Simon & Schuster.

LeDoux, J., & Phelps, E. (2008). Emotional networks in the brain. In M. Lewis & J. M. Haviland-Jones (Eds.), *Handbook of emotions* (3rd ed., pp. 159–179). New York, NY: Guilford Press.

Lerner, J., & Keltner, D. (2000). Beyond valence: Toward a model of emotion specific influences on judgment and choice. *Cognition and Emotion, 14*, 473–493.

Lerner, J., & Keltner, D. (2001). Fear, anger and risk. *Journal of Personality and Social Psychology, 81*, 146–159.

Lerner, J., & Tiedens, L. (2006). Portrait of the angry decision maker: How appraisal tendencies shape anger's influence on cognition. *Journal of Behavioral Decision Making, 19*, 115–137.

Leu, J., Wang, J., & Koo, K. (2011). Are positive emotions just as "positive" across cultures? *Emotion, 11*(4), 994–999.

Levenson, R.W. (1992). Autonomic nervous system differences among emotions. *Psychological Science, 3*(1), 23–27.

Levenson, R. W. (1994). Human emotion: A functional view. In P. Ekman & R. J. Davidson (Eds.), *The nature of emotion: Fundamental questions* (pp. 123–126). New York, NY: Oxford University Press.

Lewis, H.B. (1971). *Shame and guilt in neurosis.* New York, NY: International Universities Press

Lewis, M. (2008). Self-conscious emotions: Embarrassment, pride, shame, and guilt. In M. Lewis & J. M. Haviland-Jones (Eds.), *Handbook of emotions* (3rd ed., pp. 742–756). New York, NY: Guilford Press.

Luu, P., Tucker, D., & Derryberry, D. (1998). Anxiety and the motivational basis of working memory. *Cognitive Therapy and Research, 22*(6) 577–594.

Lyubomirsky, S., Dickerhoof, R., Boehm, J., & Sheldon, K. (2011). Becoming happier takes both a will and a proper way: An experimental longitudinal intervention to boost well-being. *Emotion, 11*(2), 391–402.

Lyubomirsky, S., King, L., & Diener, E. (2005).The benefits of frequent positive affect: Does happiness lead to success? *Psychological Bulletin, 131*(6), 803–855.

Mauss, I., Tamir, M., Anderson, C., & Savino, N. (2011). Can seeking happiness make people unhappy? Paradoxical effects of valuing happiness. *Emotion, 11*(4), 807–815.

McGregor, H., & Elliot, A. (2005). The shame of failure: Examining the link between fear of failure and shame. *Personality and Social Psychology, 31*(2), 218–231.

Mikels, J., Maglio, S., Reed, A., & Kaplowitz, L. (2011). Should I go with my gut? Investigating the benefits of emotion-focused decision making. *Emotion, 11*(4), 743–753.

Miller, R. (1992). The nature and severity of self-reported embarrassing circumstances. *Personality and Social Psychology Bulletin, 18,* 190–198.

Miller, R. (2007). Is embarrassment a blessing or a curse? In J. Tracy, R. Robins, & J. Tangney (Eds.), *The self-conscious emotions: Theory and research* (pp. 245–262). New York, NY: Gilford Press.

Miller, R., & Tangney, J. (1994). Differentiating embarrassment from shame. *Journal of Social and Clinical Psychology, 13,* 273–287.

Moran, S., & Schweitzer, M. (2008). When better is worse: Envy and the use of deception. *Negotiation and Conflict Management Research, 1*(1), 3–29.

O'Gorman, R., Wilson, D., & Miller, R. (2005). Altruistic punishing and helping differ in sensitivity to relatedness, friendship, and future interactions. *Evolution and Human Behavior, 26*, 375–387.

Öhman, A. (2010). Fear and anxiety: Overlaps and dissociations. In M. Lewis, J. M. Haviland-Jones, & L. Feldman Barrett (Eds.), *Handbook of emotions* (pp. 709–729). New York, NY: Guilford Press.

Olatunji, B., & Sawchuk, C. (2005). Disgust: Characteristic features, social manifestations and clinical implications. *Journal of Social and Clinical Psychology, 24*(7), 932–962.

Osman, M. (2004). An evaluation of dual-process theories of reasoning. *Psychodynamic Bulletin and Review, 11*(6), 988–1010.

Parkinson, B., & Illingworth, S. (2009). Guilt in response to blame from others. *Cognition and Emotion, 23*(8), 1589–1614.

Parrott, W. (1991). The emotional experiences of envy and jealousy. In P. Salovey (Ed.), *The psychology of jealousy and envy* (pp. 3–30). New York, NY: Guilford Press.

Reiss, S., & McNally, R. (1985). The expectancy model of fear. In S. Reiss & R. R. Bootzin (Eds.), *Theoretical issues in behavior therapy* (pp. 107–121). San Diego, CA: Academic Press.

Richman, L., Kubzansky, L., Maselko, J., Kawachi, I., Choo, P., & Bauer, M. (2005). Positive emotion and health: Going beyond the negative. *Health Psychology, 24*(4), 422–429.

Rothbaum, F., & Tsang, B. Y. P. (2004). Love songs in the United States and China. *Journal of Cross-Cultural Psychology, 29*(2), 306–319.

Rozin, P., & Fallon, A. (1987). A perspective on disgust. *Psychological Review, 94*(1), 23–41.

Sansone, C., Weir, C., Harpster, L., & Morgan, C. (1992). Once a boring task always a boring task? Interest as a self-regulatory mechanism. *Journal of Personality and Social Psychology, 63*(3), 379–390.

Sattler, J. (1966). Embarrassment and blushing: A theoretical review. *Journal of Social Psychology, 69*, 117–133.

Schachter, S., & Singer, J. (1962). Cognitive, social, and physiological determinants of emotional state. *Psychological Review, 69*, 379–399.

Schneiderman, I., Zilberstein-Kra, Y., Leckman, J., & Feldman, R. (2011). Love alters autonomic reactivity to emotions. *Emotion, 11*(6), 1314–1321.

Schraw, G., Wadkins, T., & Olafson, L. (2007). Doing the things we do: A grounded theory of academic procrastination. *Journal of Educational Psychology, 99*(1), 12–25.

Schwarz, N. (1990). Feelings as information: Informational and motivational functions of affective states. In E. T. Higgins & R. M. Sorrentino (Eds.), *Handbook of motivation and cognition: Foundations of social behavior* (Vol. 2, pp. 527–561). New York, NY: Guilford Press.

Shariff, A., & Tracy, J. (2009). Knowing who's boss: Implicit perceptions of status from the nonverbal expression of pride. *Emotion, 9*(5), 631–639.

Shiroy, L., & Roynoldo, R. (1988). Effect of interest on attention and learning. *Journal of Educational Psychology, 80*(2), 159–166.

Silvia, P. (2001). Interest and interest: The psychology of constructive capriciousness. *Review of General Psychology, 5*(3), 270–290.

Silver, M., & Sabini, J. (1978). The perception of envy. *Social Psychology, 41,* 105–111.

Smith, R. H., & Kim, S. H. (2007). Comprehending envy. *Psychological Bulletin, 133,* 46–64.

Smith, R. H., Turner, T., Garonzik, R., Leach, C., Urch-Druskat, V., & Weston, C. (1996). Envy and schadenfreude. *Personality and Social Psychology Bulletin, 22*(2), 158–168.

Strack, F., Stepper, S., & Martin, L. (1988). Inhibiting and facilitating conditions of the human smile: A nonobtrusive test of the facial feedback hypothesis. *Journal of Personality and Social Psychology, 54*(5), 768–777.

Sylvers, P., Lilienfeld, S., & LaPrairie, J. (2011). Differences between trait fear and trait anxiety: Implications for psychopathology. *Clinical Psychology Review, 31,* 122–137.

Szymanski, J. (2011). *The perfectionist's handbook: Take risks, invite criticism, and make the most of your mistakes.* Hoboken, NJ: Wiley.

Tangney, J. (1993). Shame and guilt. In C. G. Costello (Ed.), *Symptoms of depression* (pp. 161–180). New York, NY: Wiley.

Tangney, J. (1995). Shame and guilt in interpersonal relationships. In J. Tangney & K. Fischer (Eds.), *Self-conscious emotions: The psychology of shame, guilt, embarrassment, and pride* (pp. 114–139). New York, NY: Guilford Press.

Taylor, S. E., Klein, L. C., Lewis, B. P., Gruenewald, T. L., Gurung, R. A., & Updegraff, J. A. (2000). Biobehavioral responses to stress in females: Tend-and-befriend, not fight-or-flight. *Psychological Review, 107,* 411–429.

Thomaes, S., Bushman, B. J., Stegge, H., & Olthof, T. (2008). Trumping shame by blasts of noise: Narcissism, self-esteem, shame, and aggression in young adolescents. *Child Development, 79,* 1792–1801.

Thomaes, S., Stegge, H., Olthof, T., Bushman, B., & Nezlek, J. (2011). Turning shame inside out: "Humiliated fury" in young adolescents. *Emotion, 11*(4), 786–793.

Tompkins, S. (1962). *Affect, imagery, and consciousness. Vol. 1. The positive affects.* London, England: Tavistock.

Tompkins, S. (1963). *Affect, imagery, and consciousness: Vol. 2. The negative affects.* New York, NY: Springer.

Tomkins, S., & McCarter, R. (1964). What and where are the primary affects? Some evidence for a theory. *Perceptual and Motor Skills, 18,* 119–158.

Tracy, J., & Robbins, R. (2007a). Emerging insights into the nature and function of pride. *Current Directions in Psychological Science, 16*(3), 147–150.

Tracy, J., & Robbins, R. (2007b). The psychological structure of pride: A tale of two facets. *Journal of Personality and Social Psychology, 92*(3), 506–525.

Tugade, M., & Fredrickson, B. (2004). Resilient individuals use positive emotions to bounce back from negative emotional experiences. *Journal of Personality and Social Psychology, 86*(2), 320–333.

van de Ven, N., Zeelenberg, M., & Pieters, R. (2009). Leveling up and down: The experiences of benign and malicious envy. *Emotion, 9*(3), 419–429.

van de Ven, N., Zeelenberg, M., & Pieters, R. (2010). Warding off the evil eye: When the fear of being envied increases prosocial behavior. *Psychological Science, 21*(11) 1671–1677.

van Dijk, W., van Koningsbruggen, G., Ouwerkerk, J., & Wesseling, Y. (2011). Self-esteem, self-affirmation, and schadenfreude. *Emotion, 11*(6), 1445–1449.

Weiss, J., & Sampson, H. (1986). *The psychoanalytic process: Theory, clinical observations, and empirical research.* New York, NY: Guilford.

Weiss, R. (1973). *Loneliness: The experience of emotional and social isolation.* Cambridge, MA: MIT Press.

Williams, C., & Bybee, J. (1994). What do children feel guilty about? Developmental and gender differences. *Developmental Psychology, 30*(5), 617–623.

Williams, L., & DeSteno, D. (2008). Pride and perseverance: The motivational role of pride. *Journal of Personality and Social Psychology, 94*(6), 1007–1017.

Winkielman, P., Zajonc, R. B., & Schwarz, N. (1997). Subliminal affective priming resists attributional interventions. *Cognition and Emotion, 11,* 433–465.

Woody, S., McLean, C., & Klassen, T. (2005). Disgust as a motivator of avoidance of spiders. *Anxiety Disorders, 19,* 461–475.

Wrzesniewski, A., McCauley, C., & Rozin, P. (1999). Odor and affect: Individual differences in the impact of odor on liking for places, things, and people. *Chemical Senses, 24,* 713–721.

Zajonc, R. (1980). Feeling and thinking: Preferences need no inferences. *American Psychologist, 35,* 151–175.

Zajonc, R. (1984). On the primacy of affect. *American Psychologist, 39*(2), 117–123.

Zoccola, P., Green, M., Karoutsos, E., Katona, S., & Sabina, J. (2011). The embarrassed bystander: Embarrassability and the inhibition of helping. *Personality and Individual Differences, 51*(8), 925–929.

Zou, Z., & Wang, D. (2009). Guilt versus shame: Distinguishing the two emotions from a Chinese perspective. *Social Behavior and Personality, 37*(5), 601–604.

INDEX

Traits, emotion, 11
Trauma, 26–27
Triangle, social, 107–108
Trust, 67–68

Unconscious processes, 5–8, 76
Unhealthy anxiety, 18–19
Unintentionally embarrassing
  behavior, 35

Values, 106, 122–123
Venting anger, 90–92

Vigilance, 16
Visualizing, 76, 121–122

Wang, Jennifer, 119
Western culture, 118–119
Winning, 27–28, 58
Wishing, 71–73
Worry, 19–20
Worthiness, 56

ABOUT THE AUTHOR

Mary Lamia, PhD, is a psychologist and psychoanalyst who practices in Kentfield, California. She is also a professor at the Wright Institute in Berkeley, California. Extending psychological knowledge to the public has been her endeavor for 30 years. For nearly a decade she hosted a weekly call-in talk show, *KidTalk With Dr. Mary,* on Radio Disney stations, and her opinion has been sought in hundreds of television, radio, and print media interviews and discussions. She is the author of the 2011 Magination Press book, *Understanding Myself.*

ABOUT MAGINATION PRESS

Magination Press publishes self-help books for kids and the adults in their lives. Magination Press is an imprint of the American Psychological Association, the largest scientific and professional organization representing psychologists in the United States and the largest association of psychologists worldwide.